Audrey Healy is a freelance joulished in the *Sunday Independent* *Champion, Longford News, Westn.* ......, ...s r our, Jemma Publications and several other publications, including Dublin weeklies and trade magazines. A native of Rooskey, Co Roscommon, she is the author of two books, *St Thérèse in Ireland* and *Dubliners: What's the Story?*

Don Mullan is the author of two best-selling investigative books: *Eyewitness Bloody Sunday* (Wolfhound Press, 1997 and Merlin Publishing, 2002); and *The Dublin and Monaghan Bombings* (Wolfhound Press, 2000). He has also written/edited ten books on religious topics, including: *A Gift of Roses: Memories of the Visit to Ireland of St Thérèse* (Merlin Publishing 2001); and eight *Little Books* published in both Ireland and the USA by Columba Press and Pauline Books and Media.

Mullan has been published in all Irish national newspapers, as well as newspapers in the UK, Italy, France, USA and Brazil. His first book, *Eyewitness Bloody Sunday*, was a major catalyst in the establishment in 1998 of a new Bloody Sunday Public Tribunal of Inquiry, which is the most expensive tribunal in British legal history. The book was also the inspiration for the award-winning movie, *Bloody Sunday* (winner at the Sundance and Berlin Film Festivals), which he co-produced with British filmmakers, Mark Redhead and Paul Greengrass. He also co-produced with Greengrass the 2004 award-winning movie, *Omagh* (Winner of the San Sebastian and Toronto Film Festivals). He is currently co-producing a BBC film about *Truth and Reconciliation*.

Contacted

Testimonies of people who say the dead are alive …
and have been in touch

AUDREY HEALY
and
DON MULLAN

MERCIER PRESS

MERCIER PRESS
Douglas Village, Cork, Ireland
www.mercierpress.ie

Trade enquiries to Columba Mercier Distribution,
55a Spruce Avenue, Stillorgan Industrial Park, Blackrock, Dublin

© Audrey Healy/Don Mullan, 2005

ISBN: 978 185635 478 3

10 9 8 7 6 5 4 3 2

Special thanks to Faber and Faber for permission to quote from 'Little Gidding' from Collected Poems 1901–1962 *by T. S. Eliot.*

*Mercier Press receives financial assistance from
the Arts Council/An Chomhairle Ealaíon*

Printed and Bound in Ireland by Colour Books Ltd.

Contents

Dedication

Dedicated to a very special friend who helped me believe
that anything is possible and who always makes me smile.

Audrey Healy

And to the memory of Gary Burke who faithfully and
heroically kept a promise he made to his father in 1953
until his untimely death in 2003, aged 66.

Don Mullan

Acknowledgements

We would like to thank the following people who assisted us with the compilation and publication of this book:

Everyone who contributed their stories, as well as those who have not been included in the final selection; eight contributors asked to remain anonymous and in keeping with the format of the presentation, we have given them an alias along with their general location. We would also like to thank Lora O'Brien, Adrienne Murphy, Mary Feehan and all the staff of Mercier Press; Gary White Deer who was part of the seed idea of this book; John Scally for continuing encouragement and support; Bewley's Café, Westmoreland Street, where the idea for the book was hatched over large white coffees and sticky buns; Seamus McKinney, *The Irish News*, *The Marian Finucane Show*, RTE and all our media colleagues, both print and broadcast, who publicised our idea; Bernie Bergin for secretarial assistance; Emer Ryan and Mary Mullins for editorial assistance and advice; Seamus Cashman for invaluable support and advice in developing the concept of the book; Dr Michael Corry, Fr Brian D'Arcy, Daena Smoller, Sr Anne and Barbara Mallon who kindly agreed to be interviewed for our epilogue; County Longford librarian Mary Carletron Reynolds, Kitty Rodgers and all the staff of Longford Library for their kindness and support; Grace Brennan of Shannonside

Radio; the staff of the *Longford News*; Charlie McGettigan; RTE newscaster Bryan Dobson for launching our book; and finally to Audrey's parents Rutledge and May; to Don's family, Margaret, Therese, Carl and Emma; and to our extended families and friends for their patience and help in this project.

Audrey Healy and Don Mullan
September 2005

Introduction

The Ultimate Question

Is there life after death?
It's a question that has engaged the minds of every culture across the earth since the beginning of human consciousness. Great but now extinct civilisations such as the Incas and the Aztecs of the Americas, the builders of the Egyptian pyramids in Africa and the builders of megalithic tombs and stone circles in Europe testify to humanity's engagement with the ultimate question. In Asia, the ancient religions of Judaism, Hinduism and Buddhism grapple with the question in different ways but with a definite answer – based not on facts but on faith. Their answer is yes! Christians believe that their founder, Jesus of Nazareth, not only died but also rose from the dead and having ascended into Heaven, will return for a second time at the end of the world.

But only those who have died have the answer. The living, in many instances, live in dread of the moment when, upon drawing their last breath, the answer will be revealed in eternal nothingness or eternal life. It's a frightening thought, one that some consider morbid and many prefer to leave in abeyance. Others find it an enlightening thought, full of hope, fascination and promise.

But how do we know? Indeed, is it possible to know?

There are some who have tried to communicate with the dead through the help of mediums, clairvoyants and psychics. This is where the living try to communicate with the dead. But, if there is life after death, is it possible for those who have 'passed over' to communicate with the living? That's the fascinating question this book attempts to explore, not through scientific or academic methodology, but by allowing people from around the world tell their stories of having been 'contacted' by the living dead.

The idea for this book began in 1994 during a visit that I made with a Choctaw Native American friend, Gary White Deer, to Westminster Abbey, London. While walking through Poets' Corner, located in the south transept, Gary realised that we were literally walking over the graves of many of Britain's most celebrated writers, dramatists and poets, including Robert Browning, Geoffrey Chaucer, Charles Dickens, Thomas Hardy, Rudyard Kipling, Thomas Macaulay and the poet laureate, Lord Tennyson. To walk on the graves of those who have passed on is anathema for Native Americans and Gary was horrified at the discovery. As Gary's realisation dawned and his discomfort intensified we found ourselves at the memorial stone of the American-born nobel laureate T. S. Eliot (1888–1965). It was the inscription at the bottom of the memorial from his poem 'Little Gidding' which caught our imagination and which has become the seed for this book:

the communication
of the dead is tongued with fire beyond
the language of the living.

Can the dead communicate with the living, as Eliot seems to suggest? Indeed, the entire sentence from which the above quote is taken is more enlightening:

And what the dead had no speech for, when living,
They can tell you, being dead: the communication
Of the dead is tongued with fire beyond the language of the
living.

There have been various books written about the living trying to communicate with the dead. Often through the alleged powers of mediums, clairvoyants or psychics it is not unusual for those left behind to try to reach across the void of the beyond in an effort to reconnect with lost loved ones. This book, however, has chosen not to explore the subject of the living reaching out to the dead. Instead, we have chosen to collect stories and testimonies of people who allege that they have been 'contacted' by the dead.

My colleague, Audrey Healy, and I have endeavoured to approach this subject with an open mind. Those who shared their stories with us from around the world appear to be of a sound and rational mind. In many instances they express puzzlement and shock at what appears to be a communication from the dead 'beyond the language of the living'. Some stories are written in detail with emotions and memories evoking vivid pictures. Others are written with simplicity and some with humour. All are written with sincerity. Some describe the appearance of a dead relative, friend or stranger. Others describe an unexplained incident at a poignant moment when it appeared a lost loved one wished to communicate a reassuring message such as: 'Don't worry, I am near and at peace and still love you.' Others describe a convergence of circumstances – perhaps simple coincidence – but which they believe was a brief tangible experience of the fusion of the living and the dead.

In my own life I have had moments that certainly made me curious and have added to the wonderment of this topic.

In 1976 my best friend, Shaunie McLaughlin, was killed in a car crash in Ireland. He was twenty-one and I was twenty. The year before he died we hitchhiked through Normandy in France and visited, amongst other places, the city of Lisieux, famous for a young nineteenth-century Catholic saint named Thérèse Martin or St Thérèse of Lisieux.

Shaunie and I spent several days in Lisieux and found a wonderful welcome and hospitality there. We enjoyed exploring all the places in the city associated with the young saint who died at the age of twenty-four in 1897. We were particularly impressed by her attitude towards death. In her autobiography she wrote about her terminal illness: 'I am not dying, I am entering Life.' She went on to say that after death she would spend her Heaven doing good on earth.

The year that Shaunie died is long remembered in Ireland as an 'Indian summer'. We had uninterrupted sunshine for almost three months – quite a treat on an island renowned for overcast skies. The week before he died Shaunie said he'd like to talk to me about things that were worrying him. We agreed that he should pick me up from my football training and bring me home so I could bath and change and then we would go for a meal and a chat. I had just discovered the music of Simon and Garfunkel and before taking my bath I played for him *Bridge over Troubled Water*. As I ascended the stairs of my home to the bathroom, the song seemed appropriate given Shaunie's troubled mind.

Twenty-five years later, in 2001, the relics of the young saint were brought to Ireland and the crowds that turned out to venerate them stunned both media and religious professionals. The relics came to the city of Derry, in the north-west of Ireland, where Shaunie and I were born and grew up, and it was to there that my news editor in *Ireland on Sunday* dispatched me to do a report. By coincidence, the following day I was in Paris with several hours free before a late evening meeting. The loss of my best friend is something I still feel keenly and it being the twenty-fifth year of his death I decided to take a train from Paris to Lisieux and wander around the town, remembering the happy few days I had spent there with him.

It was, in truth, a very special and emotional visit during which I was totally absorbed in retracing our footsteps and remembering the places and experiences we shared. After several hours of walking in warm sunshine, during which I temporarily lost my way, I began to feel parched and hungry. As I found my way back toward Lisieux town centre I spotted a self-service restaurant which I entered. Having collected a tray and plate I began to survey the sumptuous fare and it was then that I stood momentarily transfixed. Softly in the background a French radio station was broadcasting Simon and Garfunkel's *Bridge over Troubled Water*.

I cannot explain the surge of emotions that charged through my being at that moment. Literally, the hair stood on the back of my neck. I gathered my food and drink and found a quiet corner in the restaurant. I am not ashamed to admit that I shed some tears. It was not the first time I had wondered if Shaunie had tried to communicate with me through music. The day he was killed I was 200 miles away on a camping holiday. Less than an hour after I had received the news that he was dead the first song I heard on a radio was Terry Jack's *Seasons in the Sun*, with the opening line: 'Goodbye to you my trusted friend …' That too had stunned me in the same way as hearing *Bridge over Troubled Water* twenty-five years later on a French radio station.

Was it coincidence? Perhaps, but I found comfort in the thought that Shaunie had, like the young Lisieux saint, simply passed from life to *life*.

On another occasion I was keeping vigil over my father who was seriously ill in hospital. The year was 1987. He awoke during what seemed to be the night's darkest and longest hour and we began to chat. He knew that he was dying and no doubt his mind was full of serious contemplation about the meaning of life and fear of the unknown.

He told me a story which, I must confess, initially caused me to wonder about the soundness of his mind. It concerned

16

an apparent apparition of his Maltese grandfather at the very moment he died in a nearby room.

Charles Zammit was a merchant seaman and chief engineer on the SS *Harrington* which sailed up the river Foyle and docked at Derry port in the north-west of Ireland during the 1880s. He met his wife, Mary Mellon, and thereafter never left the Irish city where he is now buried. They married and had six children. My father was their first grandchild and was, by all accounts, deeply loved by his grandfather, after whom he was named.

I have been told it was a common sight to see the grandfather holding the hand of his little grandson and taking him for a walk around the streets of the old walled city where they lived. There was, unquestionably, a deep bond of love and affection between them.

My father told me from his hospital bed that the night his grandfather died he came to my father, woke him up and told him that he had to leave to go on a journey and that they wouldn't see one another for a while but that one day they would be reunited. My father said he began to cry at the moment of his departure.

I sat there listening, not quite knowing how I should respond. However, in truth, I doubted what my old man was telling me and thought perhaps he was hallucinating as a result of medication. The story, however, both intrigued me and bothered me and I resolved as daybreak approached that I would visit an old grandaunt, Josie Boyle (née Zammit), whose mind was clear and sharp.

I was relieved from my duty at around 9 a.m. Without saying a word to anyone I drove to my grandaunt's home on Bishop Street, Derry. Her daughter Margaret welcomed me in and over a cup of tea I asked the old lady if she could remember the night her father died and whether anything unusual had happened.

Grandaunt Josie told me that she, my grandmother Mary Mullan (née Zammit) and other siblings were keeping vigil over their father. 'I remember,' she said, 'that at the very moment he drew his last breath, your father, who was asleep in the room next door, began to cry. I went with your grandmother to check on him and we found him standing in his cot crying sorrowfully. He was about three years old at the time.' She told me that as my grandmother gathered him into her arms she asked him what was the matter. They both were shocked when he told them that his granddad had just been in the room and told him he was going away.

Later I discovered that one of England's best-loved television personalities, botanist David Bellamy, wrote about a similar experience in his autobiography *The Jolly Green Giant*. Bellamy describes meeting his grandmother on his way home one day and how they chatted beside a flowering yucca plant, before he discovered that she had, in fact, already died by the time they met.

I have encountered other strange stories in my life which certainly made me think. What impresses me most is the fact that the people who have related these stories to me are unemotional, rational and often embarrassed to be telling them for fear that they might be considered strange or on the road to losing their marbles.

In 1998 I interviewed the fourteen wounded, or their next of kin, about their recollections of an incident known as 'Bloody Sunday'. It was a horrific event that occurred at the end of a Northern Ireland civil rights march on 30 January 1972 when British army paratroopers opened fire on unarmed civilians, killing thirteen.

One of the wounded, Joseph Mahon, then a boy of fourteen, fell in an area known as Glenfada Park where several people had been shot. To his immediate left and right lay two young men who were wounded and dying, William McKinney and James Wray. What compounded the horror and tragedy of this incident was the fact that James Wray was paralysed by the first bullet that struck him but tried to raise himself when a paratrooper walked up to him and fired a shot into his back from close range. This amounted to the summary execution of an already wounded man. Independent civilian and military eyewitness statements corroborate the testimony of young Mahon, while independent ballistic experts and forensic pathologists tested the veracity of their statements and concurred with them.

Mahon told me that he initially did not realise he was wounded and in the terror of the moment considered trying to continue his escape from the advancing paratroopers. It was then that he saw an elderly woman, holding rosary beads, standing by a window on an upper balcony. As their eyes engaged Mahon heard the old woman say, 'Son, do not move.

Pretend you are dead.' This he did and it was moments after this that he witnessed the execution of James Wray.

After young Mahon was released from hospital he returned to Glanfada Park, as he wished to meet the old woman to thank her for saving his life. He went to the balcony and knocked on the door of the apartment in which he saw the old woman. To his surprise the occupants did not know what he was talking about and said no one of that description lived there or in the apartments adjacent. Naturally, the young boy was puzzled and confused for he remembered and still remembers the incident of the old woman as having been very real.

Sometime later, it could have been months or a couple of years, Mahon was in his home and began to browse through an old family photo album. To his utter amazement he found a picture of the old woman he had encountered during Bloody Sunday. When he pointed her out to his parents they informed him that she was an old aunt who had been dead for many years. She had been ostracised by some of her Irish family for having married a British soldier. Joe Mahon, now a middle-aged man, remembers the old lady as real, has no doubt that he encountered her and credits her with saving his life.

Another of the wounded of that day, Michael Quinn, wrote a fascinating account for this book about his encounter with one of the dead while being driven to hospital.

One possible explanation is that Joe Mahon and Michael Quinn were in such an acute state of shock that their minds were playing tricks. That is, indeed, possible. Another possibility is that in moments of high energy, when sudden death and injury occur, the world of the living and the world of the spirit can connect and that some are allowed to witness the rite of passage or, as in the case of young Mahon, are protected from it since their time has not yet come.

There is, however, no definitive answer.

On another occasion I was speaking with a man in his late thirties, named Jim, who had been a former member of an illegal paramilitary organisation. He had little time for emotion or sentimentality. Jim described how one day he was working on a bridge when a workmate in his mid-fifties collapsed with a massive heart attack. Some of his co-workers ran to the man's aid and immediately tried to resuscitate him with varying degrees of desperation. Jim, however, said he was transfixed and could not move. As he watched his workmates pound on their colleague's chest, Jim kept repeating, 'It's no use, he's dead, he's dead.'

Eventually, in frustration, one of those working on their collapsed colleague raised his head and asked, 'How do you know?'

He replied, 'I felt his spirit pass through me!'

Jim described the experience as one of a cool refreshing breeze passing through his being. Again he had no rational explanation other than the fact it had happened and it was a real experience.

A longstanding friend who now lives in Australia told the following story to me. Rose was born in a rural town in

Ireland. When she had come of age she applied for and was given an apartment by the local housing authority in what were then called 'Duffy's Flats'.

Rose recalls many evenings alone in the apartment and an inexplicable feeling of well-being and of being comforted. She loved being alone there and enjoyed a serene sense of acceptance and happiness.

Eventually Rose fell in love, was engaged and after their marriage she and her fiancé planned to live together in the apartment. The evening before they were due to return from their honeymoon one of Rose's sisters visited the apartment with the intention of lighting a fire and making sure it was warm and comfortable for the newlyweds' return. However, she was overcome with a profound and tangible experience of coldness that made her feel very uncomfortable and un-welcome. She literally ran out of the apartment but did not tell anyone of her experience until after the events I am about to relate came to light.

Rose and her husband Des returned and moved in. Al-most immediately, the warm sense of being comforted, which Rose had experienced when she was alone, ended. Strange and inexplicable activities began to occur. Both she and her husband told me that at night they would lie in bed and could hear footsteps in the corridor outside their bedroom approach and the landing light would be switched on. On several nights Des jumped out of bed and quickly opened the door to check the corridor but no one was there. He would turn off the light but it would turn itself on again.

On other occasions they said they would wake up in the morning to find the waste bin from the kitchen sitting on their bed. It was not uncommon for them to either awake or return to the apartment and find furniture had been rearranged.

The young couple became so perturbed about these happenings that they sought spiritual counsel from their local parish priest. The priest had no hesitation in advising them to leave the apartment immediately, which they did. Speaking from Australia, Rose told me that the priest had told her that the May procession, led by children who had made their First Holy Communion, deliberately stopped each year to say a decade of the rosary outside Duffy's Flats because of the reported sightings of a ghost in the building over the years. When I met them in the early 1980s, Rose and Des were living in a mobile home on the outskirts of a nearby town and the events they were describing to me had happened only two years previously.

Upon investigation the priest discovered that the apartment complex where these events occurred had been built on land that housed stables a century before. He also discovered that a young stable-hand had met with a sudden and violent death when a rearing horse kicked him. The priest was convinced that Rose and Des had encountered the unquiet and unhappy poltergeist spirit of this deceased young man. It appeared that the young man's spirit had taken up residence in Rose's apartment and was happy to have Rose there but when she brought in her new husband he was jealous and became mischievous. A religious ritual was duly held and, by all accounts, there has been no recurrence. The young stable-hand has, apparently, been released from whatever impediment prevented him from moving across and, it would seem, is now at peace.

All of the above are but a few of the stories I have personally gathered. Audrey Healy and I have selected a further sixty-six stories from hundreds that we received from around the world for this, our first volume. It is important to remember that all of the stories are recounted by people who believe a deceased person has made 'contact' through a ghostly apparition, the physical manipulation of light, sound or smell, or by the convergence of circumstances that they believe is more than mere coincidence.

Our methodology in collecting these stories was simple. We began by sending out a request to radio stations and local, provincial and national newspapers. This led to a series of broadcast interviews and printed articles in which we appealed for stories and gave examples of what we had already collected. We carefully emphasised that we were not looking for accounts of people who had deliberately attempted to communicate with the dead. We only wished to hear from people who were genuinely surprised or, indeed, shocked, when they felt 'contact' had been made by those who had passed on.

The conclusion to this book is written by Audrey Healy and deals with the responses of various experts in this field. They include a religious minister, a psychiatrist, a bereavement counsellor and others who consider themselves to be alert to the 'spirit world'.

The stories Audrey and I have chosen to publish introduce the reader to a phenomenon that certainly gives pause for thought. If what many of our contributors say is true, then it is reasonable to conclude that there is further life after death; that our current lives are but transitory passages in which our spirits are contained by the limitations of our physical bodies. What lies beyond no one knows but, perhaps, the following stories might provide an insight that offers hope and consolation.

However, there is no definitive proof. Sceptics, doubters and cynics will continue to fulfil an important function by challenging and encouraging the human mind to be alert to superstition and falsity. However, many who have contributed to this book previously considered themselves to have been amongst the incredulous but are now convinced that there is life beyond living. With honesty and integrity they have shared their experiences and for that we are grateful. In the end – and it will probably always be so – whether or not one believes in the authenticity or possibility of what the contributors describe comes back to one perennial ingredient: Faith.

DON MULLAN
Co-author
Dublin, Ireland, September 2005

1

Visions

This chapter deals with actual visitations and apparitions of deceased loved ones to special friends and grieving family members. Our first testimony sets the tenor of many testimonies to follow. A deceased mother returned to her grieving child to announce there was no such thing as death. 'She told me to think of water and how it existed as liquid, as steam and as ice. It was still water, just in a different state. This is what happens to us when we die. The body dies but we exist on another level at a different vibration ...'

Paul, County Down, Northern Ireland

My mother died on my birthday thirteen years ago. She had been ill for some time. She was being cared for in a nursing home, where I visited her three days before she died. I was concerned for her and since I lived some forty miles away I appealed for an angel to be with her and to comfort her. In fact anyone who visited her – even the nurses – remarked that there was an obvious presence in the room after that day. My mother seemed to be aware of the angel as well as she kept staring in the direction of the area where we sensed the presence. She died on the following Sunday night at 9.55 p.m. My brother, sister and myself had not left her side that evening. In fact I was lying beside her on the bed with my arm around her. Unfortunately at 9.50 p.m. a nurse came into the room to tell me there was a phone call for me. I went to take the call and my mother died when I was out of the room. I was devastated. My father had died when I was six and again because I was so young I wasn't with him either.

I returned to work a few weeks later. I worked in a residential training school, and one night was in a secure unit on night duty. I started at 9.45 p.m. and usually it's hectic for the first few hours, as the young people are in locked rooms and have to 'buzz' if they need the toilet or a drink. I was on duty alone.

I was also studying and had some written work to do, so I settled in the office, started taking notes and waited for the usual fanfare of buzzers going off. Strangely this didn't happen. I remember looking up at the clock – it was 10.30 p.m. when I became aware of someone standing at the door. I looked over and there was my mother, she was radiant, glowing and she was smiling. She started to talk to me but her lips were not moving. I was frozen, paralysed but my hand was writing away on the notepad. The rest of me was unable to move, and I couldn't speak. Tears were running down my cheeks. When I 'came to' she had 'melted' away and I was left with a page of writing. It was 2.30 a.m. I had lost four hours of the night.

She told me not to worry, that she would always be close

and that there was no such thing as death as we know it. She told me to think of water and how it existed as liquid, as steam and as ice. It was still water, just in a different state. This is what happens to us when we die. The body dies but we exist on another level at a different vibration. She also used the story of the parting of the Red Sea in the Bible – that while the waters were parted the 'dead' could communicate with us, but when the sea closes over the responsibility then becomes ours and we rouse our consciousness to contact them. I was given her wedding ring on the night she died, and my mother also told me that that was how I could feel her presence – just focus on her ring. This has worked for me on many occasions.

Margaret, County Cavan, Ireland

A message was delivered to me in what I would describe as a 'vision'. It was early in the morning in my kitchen when I was seated at the table.

My eyes were open. I was gazing at the floor ahead of me as I relaxed for a few moments after breakfast. Suddenly I saw a lovely fair-haired young boy of seven or eight running towards me along a path with a hedge with green foliage and some railings to his left side. He ran his hand along the railings on his way, and said, in a lovely soft voice 'Nothing changes, only us', just at that the whole scene vanished. I was elated. I felt so privileged to be awake, and conscious of what I had witnessed. To me obviously there was a message, but strangely enough you are one of the very few people I have shared this with, possibly because I fear other people would think I was going daft. In the world we live in today – people are too busy leading their fast lives and they just don't want to know or share other experiences of this nature.

The life and death situation is always the same; it is us who change our views, our outlooks and our beliefs. They are all personal to our own being. This is why I have never spoken too much about my sighting of this beautiful young boy. I considered it personal.

Terry, County Dublin, Ireland

At the turn of the twentieth century my grandfather's siblings lived in various tenements on the Liffey quays. My grandfather John, joined the British army in 1913 and never lived on the quays. He fought in the First World War like many Dublin men and after the war joined the Irish army.

During the War of Independence in 1916 the family home on Merchants Quay was badly damaged and the family eventually ended up living at 7 Inns Quay beside the four courts.

No. 7 Inns Quay was a five-storey tenement, with a dark stairs. A few samples still exist on the quays including No. 15 Ushers Island, which is in the process of being restored because of its association with James Joyce.

During the 1930s and 1940s my grandfather was visiting his sisters at 7 Inns Quay. He climbed the dark stairs on his way to the top of the building where his sisters lived. Suddenly he saw a man coming down the stairs and beckoned him to come down. The stairs were narrow and it would have been difficult for both to pass midway on the stairs. The man came down the stairs and quietly passed my grandfather. He did not acknowledge my grandfather and continued down the stairs. My grandfather thought this was strange and turned to see the man – however he had disappeared.

My grandfather was shocked by the experience and the story lived on in the family to this day. His siblings lived out their lives at 7 Inns Quay. The building eventually became a hotel and was knocked down in the 1960s. When it was knocked down a skeleton was found under the pavement. I doubt it had any connection to the family ghost story but it does add a bit of flavour!

Thomas, Manchester, England

I was born in December 1952. I loved my granddad Thomas as he used to take me out for long walks and show me the herbal plants that cured and the wildlife around us. I was devastated when he died when I was just eight years old. I wasn't allowed to attend his funeral so on that day I was sitting outside when a dark shadow came over me. Looking up I thought I saw my granddad except he didn't have his moustache. The figure asked me why I was upset and I told him. He introduced himself as my granddad's brother Bill. He said he would take me for walks like his brother had done, so every weekend he would show up and we would chat and walk across the local fields. He used to bring, wrapped in a clean cloth, some ginger cakes and we would enjoy them on our walks.

One day my younger brother noticed Bill and asked who he was, so I told him. My brother then used to accompany us and this routine carried on for about a year, when one day Bill said he was leaving and he gave his reason as 'because you don't need me anymore, you're all right now'. We never saw him again. In 1983 I was doing my family tree and my mum mentioned my granddad's family that used to live about eight miles away. No one had been in contact with any of them so it was thought they had died off or moved to another area. I went to an old address and the family still lived there and we chatted about the family. On the wall I saw a photograph and remarked that I knew it was Bill, my granddad's brother, and enquired what became of him. I told them about his visits to us, the ginger cakes, etc. They asked when I was born and I told them December 1952. Then I was told that I could never have seen Bill as he died during the summer of 1952 after coming home after watching a cup final at Wembley. I checked the death certificate at the office and realised that he did die then, in the summer of 1952. I've told my brother this and he asked 'Who took us for walks if he was dead before we were born'? We are both convinced it was Bill. Even after mixing up pictures of the family we both picked out Bill every time.

Pamela, County Wicklow, Ireland

In 1995 my mum and I returned to Texas for another holiday at the Mayan ranch just outside the old western town of Bandera, which is about an hour north of San Antonio. We had been there several years earlier and had such an enjoyable time we decided to go back. The ranch is owned and run by the Hicks family. Don Hicks is second-generation Irish. Don and Judy run the ranch with their now adult children. Originally they had eleven children and then they adopted two local sisters whose parents had tragically died in an accident. One of their children, TJ, had been injured in an auto accident at the age of eighteen, which resulted in him becoming quadriplegic. He also had multiple organ problems – lungs, liver, etc ... My story is about TJ who was about twenty-five years of age when we arrived back to Mayan ranch in 1995.

TJ used to get about in an electric wheelchair. He had his duties to perform as his contribution to the running of the ranch. Despite his limitations he was responsible for keeping the accounts and this he did on a specially adapted computer which he operated with his mouth. He had a companion who accompanied him, helped him do whatever he needed to do and slept in his room at night should he require help. He was mentally fully functional. There was a huge family bond between all the sisters and brothers, most of whom were married and had children of their own. The family count was about fifty-six when we were there. The ranch was run by the family, and all day to day jobs were done by them. I never heard any harsh words or arguing, but they always greeted one another with hugs and smiles. Most guests only came for a two to three day break, so mum and I were quite unique in that we went for three weeks. We got to know the Hicks very well and in many ways were welcomed into their family circle.

About half way through our holiday a large group booked up the whole ranch and they organised many festivities, sports and games. It was a real fun weekend. On the Friday and Saturday evening everyone retired to the ranch saloon. TJ was there and we got to know him a lot better. Up to this we had only exchanged minimal greetings as he was usually only about during the evening barbeque. He was a good-looking fellow with the most wonderful head of wavy Irish red hair which he wore to shoulder length. That weekend he joined in with a lot of the fun and we found him to have an exceptional sense of humour. On the Saturday night in the saloon we were chatting and exchanging jokes when TJ took off his cowboy hat and put it on my head – 'Wow,' he said, 'That suits you, you look good – you can have that hat!' Well I was quite embarrassed as this drew much attention and I had always heard that a Texan never parts with his cowboy hat. Much as I would have loved that hat I replied that I couldn't possibly accept – after further pressing and my continued refusal he put the hat on mum's head and told her that she could have it with the same result. Not long after this we were going back to our cabin when TJ asked if we would like to go to Mass with him the following day and that he would come and collect us in his special vehicle that carried him in his wheelchair! Well mum and I replied that we were not really religious and had not even attended our own church for quite a while. He then invited us to go to the local rodeo in the afternoon with him. We said that we might come along but would come in our own car and see him there.

The next day dawned and mum and I decided to do some sightseeing. We did go by the rodeo but it looked very busy and we didn't think there was much chance of catching up with anyone we knew so we decided to go elsewhere. We went back to our cabin after the evening barbecue and I went to my room to bed at about 11 p.m. I read for a while and turned out the light at about 11.30. I went off to sleep right away. I woke up all of a sudden and the room was freezing cold. I couldn't understand it as the temperature had been quite warm when I went to sleep. I quickly hopped out of bed to turn off the ceiling fan and to put an extra blanket on the bed. I looked at the clock and it was only 11.45. I was mystified. I looked outside to see what the weather was like, sometimes if a sudden storm came in it would cause a cooling of the air – but nothing was changed outside. I got back into bed and cuddled up under the extra cover. Within a minute the room seemed to be warm again. I had to get out of bed and put the fan on again and get rid of the extra blanket.

In the morning we went over to the main lodge for breakfast and immediately noticed that the Hicks family were terribly distressed, most with handkerchiefs at their faces and in tears. We were told that TJ had died the night before! We were so shocked. I was even more shocked to hear that he had died at about 11.45. Was this why I got the sudden 'coldness' in my room?

We commiserated with the family and told them that as we were their only guests that day, that they should not worry about us for meals, etc. and that we would look after ourselves. They had more guests arriving in the evening and told us that the barbeque would be at the usual time. Mum and I pottered about for the day and at about 4.45 p.m. we went to enjoy some time by the pool. I am naturally a 'sinker' and therefore when I am in a pool 'swimming' I have to concentrate fully on what my arms and legs are doing. I was swimming across the pool, with my head well out of the water looking up – it was then that I saw TJ. The pool had several high oak trees at one end and TJ appeared in front of the boughs about forty feet from the ground. He was standing with his left hand in his pocket and his hat hanging down his back, his red hair was shining in the sunlight. Then I heard: 'Tell my mom I'm happy. Tell my mom I'm happy'.

I was riveted. I couldn't take my eyes off him – and then he just faded away. I looked over at where mum was sitting reading a newspaper – she hadn't noticed anything. I usually shared everything with my mum but this was so extraordinary and I guess I was somewhat in shock, so I didn't tell her. I suppose I also thought that she might think I just imagined it. When I think back I realise that how I saw TJ was completely different to when one sees someone or something in their 'mind's eye'. He was three dimensional and very real. Anyway we packed up and made our way back to the cabin to get ready for dinner. We headed for the barbeque. The family was huddled together in one area, hugging and comforting each other. 'Tell my mom I'm happy' kept repeating over and over in my head. Well I looked at Judy and Don encircled by their sons and daughters. How could I go over and intrude on their grief by repeating my experience – I didn't know how they would respond. We finished our meal and went back to the cabin. Mum was going to watch television and I decided to go for a walk. The whole time I was walking the voice pounded away in my head – 'Tell my mom I'm happy. Tell my mom I'm happy.'

Eventually I said 'OK – I will make a deal with you – if I meet her I will tell her.'

With that Judy and Don's four wheel vehicle came up a side road from the barbeque and turned back along the road I had been walking. I should and could have beckoned to them and told them – but I didn't! I continued the walk and the voice continued too. Nearly back to the cabin there was a fork in the path, straight ahead went to Judy and Don's house and the path to the right, to my cabin – I stopped ... the voice got more earnest – I felt that I could not physically take a step on the right fork to my cabin – I stood there for a few moments and then said – 'OK I'll make another bargain with you. If the lights are on in the house I will tell her but if they have all gone to bed I won't!'

It was about 9.30 p.m. at this time. Now that I had decided to go to the main house I could walk again! When I got to the house it was clear to see that all the lights were on and when I walked to the main door I could see through a side window that Don and Judy were sitting at a large family table with several of their kids. I knocked at the door and asked for Judy. When she came out I explained that I was going to tell her something that she could take on board or disregard, but that I had to tell her. When I related my experience to her she threw her arms around me and said that this had made her day, she would now be able to sleep in peace. Judy went on to tell me that the whole family had been praying all day for a sign from TJ that he was OK. I returned to the cabin but still didn't say anything to mum – I was still in a state of shock myself.

Next morning Judy came over to me while we were at breakfast, gave me a big hug and told me that she was so appreciative and had had a good night's sleep. She had told the rest of the family and they were delighted to have had the good news. They had agreed that although the family had been praying for a 'sign' from TJ, none of them could have received one because it might have been assumed that it was imagined not real. I was probably the most obvious one to get the message. I later learned that TJ's behaviour over the past weeks was unusual – he spent a lot more time with his nieces and nephews and took many of them on daily excursions in his vehicle. Another peculiar thing was that although he was not at all religious he had started attending services and only the day before had sought out the parish priest (at the rodeo) and spoke with him for over an hour. It was as if TJ knew that his time on earth was coming to an end.

I have had several experiences that led me to believe that there is an afterlife and that our nearest and dearest are not far away from us in spirit after they have passed on. TJ was the most convincing and real.

Iku, Tokyo, Japan

I am not a psychic person but sometimes I have strange experiences. My grandma was also that kind of person. When her neighbour passed away she told me she saw her ascending to the sky.

Fifteen years ago, the night of my grandma's funeral, I had a dream. I saw someone who looked like a person in silhouette but their colour wasn't black, it was orange. In my dream I was surprised and shouted, 'Who are you?' Then I woke up and to my surprise I saw a woman whose age was around fifty standing beside my futon on the tatami floor.

I had a painful cramp and the woman was going to touch softly on my belly. I was so surprised and asked her again, 'Who are you?' She now seemed surprised and began to withdraw like she was on a moving walkway and disappeared.

I was so shocked and scared. I cried and eventually fell asleep naturally. I am still not quite sure if that was my grandma or not but what I have described really did happen.

The next day I went to my workplace and told people there what I had experienced. I made everyone scared. One girl, however, who was a psychic person explained, 'Iku, that was your grandma. She knew you suffered from cramp and with kindness she came to you and was going to ease your pain.'

I asked her, 'But my grandma was nearly eighty years old when she died. The woman I saw was around fifty? How?' She replied, 'In Buddhism, when someone dies, their spirit returns to the age when they had their most wonderful period. Was

39

your grandma very happy when she was fifty?'

'Yes,' I replied, 'when she was fifty she had an extremely happy life. Her five daughters had married and she had some grandchildren.'

I still don't know if she was my grandma, but I want to believe she was.

Concerning my orange silhouette dream my psychic friend told me that the world of Buddhism is an orange colour – the colour of the sun. My cousin also had a similar experience. He told me that grandma came to him the day after her funeral. At 3 a.m. he suddenly woke up and there was grandma's face on the wall. He said he wasn't surprised, as he had seen other spirits and ghosts. He said, 'grandma, thanks for coming.' Then she smiled and faded away. My cousin saw her at 3 a.m. the exact same time as I had seen her the previous night. For some reason she visited two of her grandchildren on two consecutive nights.

I also had some other strange experiences. Just as Christians believe in guardian angels, in Buddhism we call them guardian spirits. Through a sensitive friend I learned that my guardian spirit is a woman and my ancestor from a long time ago. I believe the spirit always follows behind the human person and wants to help to protect them.

One time I was extremely depressed and I asked my guardian spirit for some help. While sleeping I heard what seemed to be a soft voice whispering in my ear just before I was about to wake up in the morning. The messages were very simple but also very helpful and encouraging such as: 'Always have the sun in your heart'; 'Don't worry, you are not alone, I am always with you'. Strangely, I could never distinguish the gender of the voice. It was neither a man's voice nor a woman's voice.

Marian, New South Wales, Australia

It was 1962 and I was eight years old. My mother had just tucked me into bed. I lay there with my eyes open, looking around the room. This was my routine before drifting off to sleep.

Suddenly, I noticed the door to my grandma's old wardrobe slowly open, seemingly by itself. To my mute horror a lady emerged slowly and began to make her way towards me. She had her arm stretched out in my direction and she looked strained and thin with stringy hair. She seemed determined to make the distance from wardrobe to bed. The closer she came the more frightened I became.

I noticed her looks; she appeared familiar and I realised later that there was a family resemblance to mum and to grandma.

This lady looked older than she probably was, with stress lines like little rivers mapping her otherwise pretty face. Her eyes had a glint of mad obsession that went beyond the polite society of an eight-year-old. She scared me.

Now she was beside the bed, with her hand outstretched to touch me. Her hands were small, with long thin fingers. This lady did not look well.

My eye caught a movement coming from the wardrobe.

Another lady emerged. She was very different although she was of slight build like the first, with very blonde hair and a white dress. She was silent but with an air of lightness and a determined peace.

She came up to the rear of the first lady and grabbed her dress. With some effort she managed to pull her back into the old wardrobe. This entire vision seemed to occur in slow motion.

At this juncture I ran out of the room, down the hall, screaming all the way. I landed safely on my parents' bed. Mum said it was a nightmare but I knew it was real.

These visions occurred at regular intervals for years. Sometimes, months would pass without a sighting. Then they would commence again as though there was no movement of time.

Years passed and I remained intrigued by the visions. Then I had an idea. Why not ask this woman, when she next appeared, who she was and what did she want from me?

This day eventually dawned. I felt the familiar cold stillness that preceded her arrival. Oddly enough, this was one occasion where she came to me without appearing from the wardrobe. She stood, in those first moments without the 'light lady'. I summoned all my courage and blurted out, 'Who are you?'

I was stunned when the vision replied, 'Anna Ross'.

'Why are you here? 'I asked.

'I don't want to leave,' she replied.

'You don't belong here anymore. There is nothing here for you now,' I told her.

'I'm too frightened to leave,' she said.

'You don't have to be frightened to leave. It's all right to go to the light. There is nothing for you to fear in the light,' I assured her.

A bit more dialogue and a few prayers later, Anna was looking fresh, unburdened and happy. All the stress was gone from her face and she was smiling. Gently she faded up and into the golden light, which at last she was able to embrace.

I felt strong as I relayed the experience to my now ageing mum. She went pale on hearing the name Anna Ross. 'That was your grandma's cousin, they were close as young women. Fancy that.'

Eventually these experiences merged into fond memories. So much so, that I wrote a piece of poetry to honour Anna and completed a rather simple painting of her. The poetry and painting were symbols to remind myself of the vulnerability of life and how we all need someone.

In 2003 as I was at my computer, tidying up and going over old pieces of poetry, I came across the poem *The Sorrows of Anna Ross*. All of a sudden, in a split second, everything in my line of vision changed. There was Anna in a garden with three fellows of her time and two youngish women. They were laughing in this beautiful place and looked so happy. Then she stood still for a moment and turned to face me. It was like she knew something.

To her friends she said, 'A descendant has written a poem about me.'

Her prettiness had returned and she appeared flattered

that someone cared. The dress she now wore was a pale cream with little yellow flowers dotted all over it.

Whether she heard me or not, I don't know but I replied, 'I will tell people about you, Anna, I promise.'

Abby, Wellington, New Zealand

Sometime in the late 1980s my sister's husband died of a heart attack/stroke in New Zealand. My brother-in-law who was from the UK, was more than twenty-five years older than my sister. At the time of his death, he had been living on his own in a city some hours drive away from their home in the country. It was decided that his body would be returned for burial in the local rural cemetery near the home he had shared with my sister. In accordance with his wishes there was to be a graveside ceremony but not a religious service as he was known to be atheist. My brother and sister and I travelled to the location for the funeral. The night before the funeral my sister and I stayed up the road in a neighbour's house.

When I awoke the next morning I recalled waking in the night and having a strong impression of a face (or person) hovering on one side above where I was sleeping – to my right or left, not directly on or above me. The best way to describe it was like seeing an oval portrait of an elderly person in the space above me in the room. I was sure it was my brother-in-law, who would have been over seventy at the time of his death. Later my brother came across from the family home where he had stayed the night and asked me what my brother-in-law looked like as he had never actually met him. 'Was he slight and stooped?' he asked. I said yes, this did describe him. He then said he had woken in the night and he was sure he'd seen someone walking down the hall of the house who looked like this and had a walking stick.

Later that day we went to the cemetery for the graveside service and I was surprised to learn that my brother-in-law – whom I thought was a native of Yorkshire, had actually spent his younger years in Belfast, Northern Ireland and attended a Christian Brother's school.

My brother (who was not a church-goer) thought he had been imagining things. On my return to my home town however I spoke about what had happened with my parish priest, an Irishman. He listened and said 'Well, the Irish do believe that the soul of a person who has died does sometimes go in search of prayer or is restless'. After that I had a Mass said for my brother-in-law. Over the years that image of a man in search of prayer for his soul has stayed with me. I have never seen any ghosts since, nor communicated as such with the dead. However I have in recent years been involved in family tree work and from time to time at church, said a prayer for anyone in the family tree who died and whose soul may not have been prayed for.

Carol, Washington, USA

My grandmother died when I was thirteen years old and I remember the day vividly. I was in the eight grade and it was a school day. My friends and I had gone to the local bakery for our lunch. Just as we were opening the door to the bakery, I felt as if my whole body was losing its strength, I could actually feel my spirit leave and then return a moment later.

I looked at my friend Sherry and told her I had to go home because my grandmother had died. She just laughed and said 'that's a terrible thing to say just to get out of taking a test in science class'. I turned around and began walking home. As I came to our street, where we had lived with my grandmother for many years, I saw my father leave in his car in a hurry.

I continued walking to the house and as I walked up the front steps to the door, I could feel my grandmother's absence and I felt so alone. I opened the front door and called out to my mother. When I saw her all I could say was 'Grandma died'.

She asked how I knew and I told her. I'm not sure she ever believed me.

Three weeks after we buried my grandmother, I was getting into bed and was just reaching for the lamp to turn the light out when I saw her standing at the end of my bed. She was smiling at me. She told me that she hadn't had a chance to say goodbye and to tell me how much she loved me. She also said that no matter where I was, I would never be without her, that she would always watch over me. Then she was gone.

I was terrified and screamed for my mother as I tore down the stairs. When I got to my mother's bedroom she looked terrified too. I told her what I had seen and she told me that grandmother had visited her also.

To this day, I can still see my grandmother's face and her smile when I am sad or just feeling lonely. I do feel that she is still beside me.

This happened in 1963, I was thirteen, and I am now going to be fifty-five years old. I am blessed that God has given me my own grandmother as my guardian angel.

Dylan, Somerset, England

In the mid 1970s I lived in a village north-west of the city of Bath in England. Opposite our home was my friend's house who had an attached allotment by the side of their property. Most days my friend's father would work in this allotment tending to his vegetables and plants, and if he spotted us, he'd always give us a wave. One day my younger sister, my mother and I left our house to go to school. My friend's dad was as usual, sitting in his garden, the sun glistening on his glasses. This is what caught our attention. We all waved at him and shouted hello. He waved back and tipped the flat cap he was wearing. We then continued off to school.

Later that day, after returning from school, I went over to see my friend as I was worried about him because he wasn't at school that day. My friend appeared at the door with tears in his eyes. Concerned I asked what was wrong and he said that his dad had died the night before.

It was comforting to think that death is not the end and that even after his passing he was still doing what he loved best.

Marion, Northampton, England

I had just moved to Northampton when after two weeks things started to happen. I was watching the television when I noticed my lamp dimming down, then back up again. This happened twice. It was as if someone was playing about with a dimmer switch. I knew instantly there was a presence. All sorts of goings on then started; I didn't mind but wondered who it could be. On another occasion I was in the living-room, trying to read the tarot. I unwrapped the cards out of the silk wrap. I placed the wrap on the settee with me and the cards on the floor. Before I carried on I went to make a cup of tea, on my return something caught my eye, on the hall floor was the silk wrap!

My television had a mind of its own, it would either channel hop or come on by itself when on standby. This went on for two days, then it stopped as quickly as it started.

2003 was a very hot summer and I had all my windows open a little. When I entered the kitchen I heard a loud bang come from the living-room. I quickly entered the living-room and one of the windows had banged shut. This window was about 3ft by 3ft double-glazed and damned heavy, no breeze could have slammed it closed. Next day the kitchen window slammed shut so I went in and opened it, no sooner was I back in the living-room than the kitchen window slammed shut again. This time I went and opened it asking the spirit not to do it again. The spirit obviously listened because it never did happen again. But this time I was wondering (I was very anxious) who it was. It was July 2003 on a Saturday evening; I had been brushing my hair in the bathroom. As I turned to leave, peeping from the bathroom door frame a spirit boy's face was staring at me. I was fascinated and intrigued by him. He was transparent, aged eighteen years old, his hair was short with a fringe. It was his hair colour that blew me away, a very white blonde colour. I was looking at him for about five seconds before he disappeared. I was adamant I didn't know him. By now my curiosity was on a high. Who was he? What did he want with me? I really did believe I would never get my answers. I was wrong!

It was about five weeks later when I was looking at the bathroom door frame and I asked 'But who are you?' Immediately the name 'Steven' came into my head and I went to get a photo album and just knew. The photo was my nan's second wedding and it was also my seventeenth birthday, 11 August 1979.

As I was looking at the photo I saw Steven, my ten-year-old cousin, standing in the front line. My eyes moved along a little and suddenly widened as I sat looking at Mark. It was him! He was only about nine years old at the time but everything else was exactly as I had previously seen him. Mark was my nan's second husband's only grandson. The wedding was the one and only time I had seen Mark and he was never mentioned again until the mid-1980s. Mum told me Mark had been killed in a car crash, aged eighteen. Had the name 'Mark' come into my head and not 'Steven' the connection probably would never have happened as I have a cousin Mark but no photos. The spirit world can have some strong ways of making the connection but I was given my answer.

Jane, Hertfordshire, England

My husband of almost thirty-six years died suddenly of a heart attack at work and we didn't have time to say goodbye. John died in February 1979 and the next Christmas my youngest daughter, then aged eighteen, and I were opening our gifts to each other. There was a snapping sound and we found that a favourite glass of my husband's, a wine glass, had broken. The top had completely come apart from the stem. I still have not had it repaired. It is a very thick glass, an unusual one that has been in his family for many years. No one had touched it. It was behind glass in a unit and apart from my daughter and myself there was no one else in the house and it was on a Christmas morning. My husband loved Christmas.

The other thing is that on the day of the funeral I went to put on my eternity and engagement rings and as I picked up my eternity ring it split in half. I took it to the jewellers some weeks after and had it tested. There was no explanation as there was no weakness in the ring. I have since had it joined up and have always worn it as a chain since then.

Also my three daughters and myself have all seen my husband. He came to me in a shopping centre dressed as I had often seen him. I also hear his voice.

I had known my husband since I was seventeen, married at twenty, widowed at fifty-six. I am now eighty-one and still love my husband as deeply as I did at seventeen.

Michael, County Derry, Northern Ireland

My story begins in Glenfada Park, Derry on a day in 1972 that became known as 'Bloody Sunday'. I had been sheltering from the gunfire in nearby Rossville Street where people were being killed and wounded at a barricade by members of the first battalion, the Parachute Regiment (the Paras). The body of a young man named Michael Kelly was being carried from the barricade through Glenfada as the same group of Paras entered to continue their killing.

I ran from where I was sheltering and had almost reached the exit when I was hit in the face, the bullet exiting through my nose. As I tumbled forward from the force of the bullet, I could see the head of someone to my right hitting the kerb. I remember thinking I wasn't the only one shot. The person I saw being shot I believe was another young man named Jim Wray.

I kept moving out of Glenfada Park and was helped to nearby Blucher Street where I received first aid treatment from two members of the Knights of Malta ambulance corp, Eibhlin Lafferty and Pauline Lynch, both of whom I knew but neither of them recognised me. I recall not wanting to lie down to be treated and asking that a car be got to take me to hospital. A white mini was quickly produced and I was put in the back. From Blucher Street we turned into Westland Street heading up the hill to the Creggan Estate where the Knights of Malta ambulance was stationed.

As we began going up the hill, one of the two men accompanying me turned and said that someone 'up there' must have been looking out for me. I hadn't thought how lucky I had been; I was busily trying to make out how much of my face was gone. I could see a hole in my nose where the bullet had exited and was not sure what else was gone.

As I was doing this I looked out the side window of the car and noticed a figure turning slowly round, looking back in the direction of Rossville Street, where the shootings had taken place. I remember thinking that he was safe. I didn't know his name but I recognised him as I had seen him around.

The next morning, in hospital, I was given a copy of the *Irish News* newspaper. It carried photographs of thirteen people killed by the Paras the day before. The same young man whom I'd seen at the top of Westland Street, turning around in the direction of Rossville Street, was amongst them. His name was John Young. I couldn't believe it. I recall saying to the person who gave me the newspaper that he couldn't be amongst the dead as I had seen him in Westland Street. According to reports, John Young had been killed at the barricade in Rossville Street, alongside Michael Kelly, a few minutes before I had been shot.

I can't explain what I saw. I have a very clear recollection of the event. It wasn't a case of being traumatised or semiconscious. It could well be a case of mistaken identity, but that's not how it felt then.

Perhaps he was going home.

2

Through a Child's Eyes

This chapter contains stories involving children, some of whom claim to have seen or conversed with a deceased person, later identified as a grandparent, relative or friend. It also contains stories of deceased children whose parents believe have remained close and supportive.

The fact that children are generally free of the cynicism that often manifests itself in adults makes some of these stories and testimonies particularly intriguing.

Paul, Alderney, Channel Islands

My wife Lisa spent much of her childhood living with her mother and grandparents as her father had to work away to boost finances. At this time a special relationship developed between Lisa and her grandmother, which was clearly evident to me at the time. Lisa and I got engaged some years later. Sadly, six months before we got married, her grandmother died but not before she spoke at length about how she dearly looked forward to Lisa having a child of her own and how much love this child would receive.

However while we were upset that this could never be, a strange thing happened when my daughter was four years old and on her own watching a Disney video whilst we were out of the room. Our living-room had two glass French doors and it was through these that our daughter came to find us and claimed she saw an old woman smiling at her. We of course at first laughed this off but after quizzing my daughter lightly she described her in great detail despite not having been told of her great-grandmother's characteristics previously. To this day, due to the clear innocence of our child my wife and I believe that this was something that can only be regarded as absolute reality.

Jim, County Derry, Northern Ireland

When I first met my wife she was a single mother with a young daughter. This fact never bothered me and within ten months we were married. In 1998 my wife discovered that she was pregnant, but unfortunately she miscarried after sixteen weeks.

I was with her when she was admitted to hospital but I wasn't aware of how ill she was. After she was admitted I went back home to fetch her an overnight bag. While I was driving home my wife prematurely gave birth to our baby son whom we named Liam Thomas.

During this time our daughter was staying at her grandmother's. She was sitting watching television when she suddenly called, 'Who's that baby crying?' Before her grandmother could answer her the phone rang. It was a nurse from the hospital looking to speak with me, so my mother-in-law passed on my telephone number.

I was at home putting some things into a bag when the phone rang; the nurse told me that my wife was asking for me. I quickly finished packing and drove back to the hospital.

When I entered the ward the nurse met me in the corridor. She told me that my wife had miscarried. I couldn't believe it. I just wanted to see my wife and make sure that she was all right. A lot of tears were shed by both of us. After a few minutes the nurse asked if we would like to see our son. When she brought him in he was laid out on his side, in a little basket. He was fully formed and was no more than the size of the palm of my hand. We named him Liam Thomas, after both of our fathers. At sixteen weeks my mother-in-law could see a resemblance between Liam Thomas and I. Even our local priest couldn't believe how well developed he was for a baby at sixteen weeks.

Two years had passed and we agreed that I should apply to adopt my wife's daughter, who by this time was calling me 'daddy'. The battle to adopt her wasn't going to be easy. The natural father, who never wanted to know his daughter, objected to me adopting her so we had to take it through the courts, something that we were not prepared for. Some days we spent up to nine hours in the corridors of the courthouse praying for the right outcome. Like my wife, I constantly prayed to our son to help us just get through another day in court. We were always running to courts, solicitors and social workers – so much so that our everyday life was taken over with all the legal work. It was a very stressful time for us as a family; our life was basically put on hold until the adoption was dealt with.

One morning at breakfast our daughter said that she had been talking to Liam Thomas. She looked at us so innocently and said 'everything is going to be all right'. After two years I was finally able to adopt our daughter with the courts' and social workers' blessings.

We had never really got over losing our son, but with the help of prayer we were able to accept it more. One night while we were watching a late film my wife fell asleep on the settee. I felt that I too was going to fall asleep but then as clear as day my son appeared to me. He was about three years old with fair hair and just like any normal child. He smiled at me and asked me to tell his mother that he was happy and for her to let him go. He stayed there for a little while, then he was gone as quickly as he had appeared. To me it was as if he was with us through all the hard times and now it was time for him to go. At first I began to doubt what had just happened but then deep down something told me not to doubt. I told my wife what had happened although I felt like a right fool. I knew that it had happened. We cried for a while, then she told me that she had never let go of him and wished that he were still alive today. We never really talked about it again and I never told any one else what I had seen.

Last year my wife's aunt who lived in England was very ill. All the time she was ill she couldn't get out of the bed and could only move her head slightly. Her family had been keeping a bedside vigil when one night they noticed her smiling. One of her daughters asked what she was smiling at. Her answer stunned the room into silence. She smiled again and said that a wee fair-haired boy was there and that it was Liam Thomas.

Neither my wife nor I had ever told anyone about our experience. Therefore no one would ever have known that he had fair hair.

I believe our son is watching over us and will always be at our side, during the good times and the bad.

Michelle, County Longford, Ireland

I was twelve years old and at boarding school when I awoke early in the morning after feeling a weight on the end of my bed. I sat up and to my surprise there was a man sitting there looking at me. Strangely enough I was not worried about this. He then spoke. 'I am your granddad and I came back to see what you looked like,' he said. I nodded my head and lay down again and went back to sleep.

One evening in the summer about six months after this had happened, the family were all together for tea. We were talking about strange things that had happened to people and I told my story. Everyone said that it must have been a very vivid dream, then granny asked what he looked like. I said that he was very tall, had a long coat with a cane with a dog's head on it and a hat but I could not see his face.

Then the mood changed and granny got upset, because I had described what my granddad had been buried in and I could not have known because I was just three years of age when he died and was not at the funeral.

Joe, County Kerry, Ireland

In 1998 my brother-in-law passed away at a young age from cancer. Not long after the funeral, some members of his family were in the sitting-room and a young grandchild aged four, pointed to her nanny and said 'Look nanny, grandda is sitting beside you and he's laughing, and he has his arm around you'. My father, his grandfather, had passed away in 1978.

Some people reckon that children are more sensitive to spirits – who knows?

I had another experience which I have to say was very pleasant and reassuring. In March 1999 my mother-in-law died from cancer. A couple of days after the funeral as we were coming home from the pub, we decided to put on a tape. As it turned out, it was her favourite song *No Matter What* by Boyzone. Just as soon as the song started we got this over-powering strong smell of roses. We did have a few drinks but there's no way that this was drink induced. It lasted around the same length as the song. It's something that I'll never forget, a sense of peace, beautiful, even our two children got the same aroma.

I can only conclude from these events that there is an afterlife somewhere out there, a better existence, peaceful, trouble free – in other words Heaven. I firmly believe this, but to try and understand the meaning of life is something that is presently beyond us.

Winifred, County Dublin, Ireland

A couple of days after my mother's funeral I went down to her empty house to tidy up a bit. I hoovered the hall and the stairs and did some other bits and pieces before leaving.

Prior to her death she was very close to my daughter who was then aged six. She would make up little plastic bags of about twelve smarties – she knew I didn't want my daughter to eat too many sweets – and give them to her when she visited.

A couple of days after the first visit to my mother's house I called down again, this time with my daughter. Just as I opened the door, there in the middle of the hall floor was a little bag of Smarties.

I had already hoovered the hall and would have seen them if they had been there previously. I believe that she placed them there for my daughter.

Also, a few weeks after her death I was awakened by my father's voice calling me saying 'Winifred, your mammy's home'. He had died ten years previous. I was really struck by this, as he would not have used the phrase 'home'.

Richard, Gloucestershire, England

My father died suddenly some years ago. I was distraught at his death but found great relief when he appeared to me in a dream and told me that he was all right and that I should not be sad.

This of course could be explained by a psychologist as my thoughts and imagination being upset and wayward. However the following is not so easy to explain. Nine months to the day after my father had died my son was born. His resemblance to my father was astounding and was commented on by everyone who knew him. When my son was about three years old we – my wife, son and daughter – moved in with my mother as she was finding it difficult to manage.

Soon afterwards my mother, my wife and I were in the kitchen. My son was outside playing with his bike. Then he suddenly appeared at the door and said 'Where did he go?' I asked who he meant. He replied 'that man, he helped me mend my bike then he came in here.' We were a little alarmed and I went outside to see if there was anyone around but found no one. My wife, mother and I discussed this event and to say the least found it peculiar but as time went by we thought no more of it.

However some weeks later we were all in the lounge going through some of my father's audio tapes. We had never played them until now as we thought it would be too upsetting.

I put a tape on and my father's voice came from the recorder at which point my son who had certainly never heard my father's voice, exclaimed 'that's the man.' I asked what he meant. 'That's the man who helped me with my bike.' We just looked at one another in absolute astonishment. It was such an emotional moment and was quite beyond our understanding. My son who is now in his twenties, does not remember these events, but my wife and I do. How could we ever forget?

Leah, Dorset, England

I would like to relate a happening or many happenings to my son who is now fifty-seven and a strong healthy man. He was just five or maybe six when the story I am about to tell happened. He said 'mum; please leave the light on in my bedroom'. My wife, God bless her, now dead and at peace with the world, said 'Why son? You never have the light on'.

'It is for the lady, she is little and old. She comes through the window, comes to my bed, smiles and then goes out through the wardrobe.'

'Darling I think you are having funny dreams, are you not afraid?' she asked.

'Oh no mum she is a nice old lady, always smiles before she leaves, she always wears the same black clothes and a black big scarf.'

My wife asked how many times this had happened.

He replied, 'I do not know mum. I go to sleep after she has gone.'

My wife was so sure that the old lady was her mother after she had got over the initial shock. Her mother died before our son was born.

3

A Stranger Calls

Some readers may recall being taught as children that God gifted each person with the presence of an angel, a spiritual being, imagined with wings, who was a personal guardian. As adults, with developed and complex minds, the simple faith and acceptance of a child can be buried under the accumulation of logic, rational thinking and acquired cynicism.

However, while we may no longer think of angels as great winged creatures who walk in our shadow or who hover invisibly above our shoulders, many have encountered good and caring beings who have emerged from a crowd to offer help and support in a moment of great need.

The throw away phrase, 'You're an angel' may not, in fact, be very far from the truth, if some of the following stories are to be believed.

Margaret, Lancashire, England

During the Second World War I served in the Women's Royal Naval Service – most of the time spent in Londonderry and later in Plymouth. When in Plymouth I was transferred to Cornwall for a brief spell. Being due for home leave I had to make my way in the government enforced blackout to start my journey to the local railway. This I'd never used before, so I was surprised to find it situated at the side of a hill with no brick buildings around it. The only access appeared to be two large white double gates. I passed through these, only to find myself on a railway track a few hundred yards from a fast express oncoming train.

In the total blackness I could see no sign of life and I uttered a feeble 'help'. But, then I saw two arms reach out for me and gently lift me to safety – as light as a feather – on to the platform. Then they vanished! Amazingly, I could see neither face nor feet only the spiritual being wearing what once he would have worn on earth – a man's check shirt and beige corduroy trousers which were popular in the 1940s, especially with manual workers.

Ted, Algarve, Portugal

During the late 1950s I was home in Cork on leave from sea and was awaiting my next posting to Kranjt Singapore station. It had been a typical wet dreary late November day but by eleven o'clock there was just a gentle mist and my father asked me to go to the small corner shop for some stamps and cigarettes and to give our cocker spaniel his daily run.

On leaving the shop we turned to go home, along the street of terraced houses and small front gardens – there was no traffic, no noise, just an eerie stillness and a strange glow from the street lamps through the midnight mist.

Suddenly the dog stopped at the gate of a house, raised his head and howled loudly, then shot off at high speed for home. As I drew level with the small gate and garden, I wondered what had caused him to react like that. Then I saw it – just six feet away, inside the small gate, a very clear image of a tall man dressed in a long coat, holding a young woman dressed in a wedding-gown. The scary thing was the unearthly glow from head to toe of both images. Needless to say my knees began to knock and I broke out in a cold sweat – so much for all your seafaring and world travel – this was something else! I soon took the hint from the dog and shot off home. 'You've gone deathly pale and look as if you've seen a ghost,' said dad, 'and the dog nearly tore down the door to get in and is hiding under the table.'

The following day at midday I went back to the shop. I paused outside the terraced house and wondered if it could have been a trick of the light? I noticed that the front garden was overgrown and the house was vacant.

'No one stays there very long,' said Miss O'Donoghue. 'The shopkeeper there says the place is haunted by a coachman and the daughter of the big house – seems she ran away and married him against the wishes of her parents.'

Years later, back from sea and now working in the local newspaper, I was sitting having a quiet drink in a local pub and heard a couple telling a story to a group of teenagers. They thought it was so funny. 'Ghosts! Don't be daft! This is the 1960s!'

When the teenagers had left I asked the couple to tell me their ghost story … I was amazed to hear an exact repeat of my story, same house, same street but this time the ghost passed through the closed gate … needless to say the couple were relieved to meet someone who had experienced their sighting.

By an odd coincidence the former owner of that house was also in the pub that night. He informed us that they decided to move out and try and sell the property, as they had many strange experiences – late night door banging, footsteps going upstairs, even though the front door had been bolted. The house was built on a part of the land of the big house – the old stables were about 200 yards away and were probably the coachman's quarters.

Victoria, Dorset, England

When I moved into my home nearly sixteen years ago, it was a brand new house so I did not expect any 'goings-on'.

Things started happening just a few weeks after moving in. My partner came home from work, one night, about 2 a.m.; I always left the lounge light on, when I went to bed. As he pulled into the driveway, the lounge curtains were slightly open and started to close very slowly, he thought I was up waiting for him to come home. I was sound asleep in bed, as were our two children. He woke me up, just to make sure I really was asleep.

After this things got steadily worse. We used to hear footsteps along the landing in the early hours, quite a few times we got up thinking it was one of the children but there was nobody there. The lounge door would open on its own and there was always a strong smell of perfume. This went on for quite a few weeks. Then my daughter, who was two and a half at the time, started talking to someone, but there was nobody there. She also started doing drawings in thick black felt pen, and the house was always cold.

All this came to a head one day. Although I was very frightened, I did not know who to turn to for help. I thought people might think I was going mad. My son, who was just a year old at the time, was sitting on the lounge floor playing when all of a sudden, a carriage clock that was on the fireplace 'flew' off just missing him. With this, I grabbed him and put him in his pushchair. I went to get my daughter so I could leave the house. She stood at the top of the stairs, talking to 'fresh air'. I kept calling and calling her, she just ignored me and carried on talking. With this I ran up the stairs, grabbed her and got out of the house.

I was very frightened and went to a friend's house a few streets away. We left the children in her lounge while we were in the kitchen, talking about it. She had a small round glass table, tucked away in the corner. All of a sudden there was a loud crash, the children were shouting and screaming. We ran into her lounge. Her glass table had been broken, the middle piece of glass was sticking up in the air in a point. It had gone into her youngest son's back; he needed three stitches. Her eldest son, who was thirteen at the time, could not explain what had happened and was crying. He said the younger ones were nowhere near the table. They were standing in the middle of the room talking and eating sweets, and her son just 'flew' backwards and landed on the table.

When I came home I was too frightened to go into my house so I called in at a neighbours who was a regular church-goer. I told her what had happened, along with everything else. She did not hesitate in calling her priest; he came straight out to see me. I explained to him what had happened and what had been happening in my home. He said it sounded like the spirit had followed me to my friend's home and I had upset it by talking about it. He came in and blessed my home, and took the drawings my daughter had done.

All was quiet for a few weeks, then things started happening again. This time I did not hesitate and called a vicar who came to my home two days later. On arriving on my doorstep, he refused to come in on his own but did not say why. He phoned for another vicar to accompany him. They once again blessed the house, but this time, blessed myself and the children as well.

Again all was quiet for a few months, then the lounge door started opening and there was a smell of perfume. But now, I was not just frightened but angry as well. Why was this happening to me? This was a brand new house, these things just don't happen in new houses.

Whenever my sister came to my home she used to say how cold it was, even in the heat of summer. Quite a few times I got so angry I used to shout at whatever it was to 'leave us alone', 'stay away from my children', then I noticed the more I shouted at it, the worse things seemed to be getting.

My son was asleep one day on the settee and I sat there with him, watching television. All of a sudden I saw this white object, moving towards us. My first instinct was to run out of the room but I knew I could not leave my son lying on the settee, so I just sat and stared at it, as it slowly started moving towards the window and disappeared.

I rang the vicar and told him what was going on and that I had had the house blessed twice already, but it kept coming back and I was very frightened.

He came out with his wife and brought some holy water. He told me not to acknowledge the spirit no matter how hard that was and not to shout at it. Every time I heard something or if something happened I was to turn the television up or put headphones on and listen to music, anything, but not to shout or talk to it as this gives it energy and that's why things had become worse. He blessed the house again but this time with holy water. He blessed me and the children, then we all said some prayers. I think the neighbours thought I was going mad, all these vicars turning up on my doorstep. He said as this was the third time the house had been blessed, if it returned, I was to let him know and he would get in touch with another vicar who would come and perform an exorcism.

Everything had been quiet for about seven years before I started child minding last October. Six months ago I started looking after a baby and whatever it is has come back. It all started with just a 'feeling' that someone was in the room with me; my daughter who is now fifteen picked up on it first. Quite a few times she has run downstairs from her bedroom frightened saying she can sense someone in her room with her. I told her it was probably either her nan or grand-dad watching over her, who we lost six and seven years ago, but I knew inside it was not. I've felt it as well and things are getting worse once again.

Three weeks ago I was at home on my own. My children were out for the evening with their dad. At 10.30 there was a terrible crash upstairs. My first thought was that something had come through the ceiling from the attic. It was that loud. As I was frightened, I rang the boys and their dad on my partner's phone. His first reaction was to tell me to leave the house. I said I had nowhere to go at that time of night. I had just had a bath and my clothes were upstairs. He told me to go and have a look while he was on the phone. I looked in all the bedrooms. There was nothing there. When I reached the bathroom all the toothbrushes and toothpaste were lying on the floor. The container in which they were held was still in its place.

I came back downstairs and watched television while I waited for the boys to come home. Half an hour later it turned cold so I went and made two hot water bottles to keep warm.

The next day my partner left with the children to visit my in-laws for a few days. I could not take the time off work, so I stayed behind on my own. Tuesday was my day off and I decided to decorate my son's bedroom while he was away. About 9.30 p.m. that night I was still upstairs clearing up. I had a horrible feeling I was not on my own, yet I was alone in the house. That night I slept downstairs on the settee with the table lamp on. When I got up in the morning I tried to pull the lounge door open, but it would not budge; it felt like someone was holding it from the other side, after a few minutes it released. I work from home and that day my sister called in and commented on how cold it was in the house. Outside it was a beautiful summer's day. I told her what was happening. She told me to phone the vicar but before I did this I wanted to find out what it was and why it was happening again. I phoned the spiritualist church. They gave me a phone number of a spiritualist medium. I rang him and left a message. On Wednesday night I slept downstairs again as I was not brave enough to sleep upstairs on my own. Around 4.30 a.m. I was woken up by a bang upstairs, then I could hear movement in my bedroom. I got up and switched the television on. I made a cup of tea and waited for daylight. As I went to walk out the front door that morning a book flew off the shelf above my telephone, just missing me. I lost my temper and shouted at it 'why don't you start throwing books at me now, why are you doing this?'

When I got home the spiritualist medium phoned me. I told him what was happening and what had happened in the past. He asked how many people were in the house at night and what my address was. He said he would see what he could do and to ring him on Sunday morning if things had not quietened down and he would come to the house.

The next few days and nights were quiet. I rang him on the Sunday and he asked how things were. I told him everything was quiet. He said if things started happening again to ring back and he would come round. I asked him if he knew what it was and why only myself and my daughter seemed to be picking up on it. He said it was a man, a woman and a little girl, that the man's name was Fred and he seemed to attach himself to girls. That's why we were able to pick things up easier.

That night, Sunday, my son had a friend sleep over. I got up to use the bathroom at about 2.45 a.m. As I came out of the bathroom I turned to go into my room and noticed someone standing in the doorway of my son's bedroom with their back to me. Thinking it was my son's friend waiting to use the bathroom I carried on into my room. I suddenly realised that nobody had gone into the bathroom so I went and had a look in my son's room. Both of them were in bed fast asleep. Neither had been out of bed.

All was quiet on Tuesday evening; I left my daughter downstairs watching television and went to bed. At around 11.30 p.m. she woke me up frightened and asked to sleep in my bed. She said she felt someone downstairs with her, it was horrible so she ran upstairs to her room and it had followed her in there.

At 5.40 a.m. I got woken up by my son. As he was lying in bed he could see the bathroom door swinging to and fro on its own. It was the first time he has experienced anything. I brought him downstairs. I am told spirits or poltergeists are attached to young children and it's funny how it's all started again after many years when I recently began looking after a baby.

People have asked me why I have not moved. I would

love to move and have a quiet life but I must get rid of my 'visitors' first as I am told you can take them with you.

Ciara, County Derry, Northern Ireland

I want to tell a story which happened in my family – a story that plays an important role in my life. I believe that if this did not happen, my brother and I, and my son, probably would never have existed.

The incident happened one January in the early 1970s. My parents had just met at a local pub called the Railway Tavern the weekend before, and daddy asked mammy out on a date. She was already seeing someone, but wasn't really serious about him, so she agreed to let my daddy take her to the pictures. Daddy picked her up and off they went in his car for their date.

As the evening progressed, gale force winds strengthened outside. There was a nasty storm brewing up. But of course, mammy still had to be left home, whatever the weather was doing! However, to reach where she lived meant driving through some countryside. They were approaching her home, on a part of the road known locally as Mc Farland's Brae, when they spied an old lady standing in the middle of the road. She was wearing clothes that my mammy remembers her grandmother wearing – a long dark skirt, and a hooded cape. She was frantically waving a lit oil tillie lamp. My daddy slammed on the breaks, the old woman stepped to the side of the road, and there right in front of them – just past a dip on the road – was a tree that had been blown across the road by the gale force winds. My daddy just got the car stopped in time.

They were both very shook up, and after a brief moment, their attention turned to the whereabouts of the old lady with the tillie lamp. Mammy was thinking to herself that surely an old woman should not be out in the middle of the road on her own on such a violently stormy night, but she was gone. She was nowhere to be seen. There were no gates or houses at that part of the road that she could have gone to – just ditches alongside the road. There was no trace of her.

That night my daddy learned that a man he played football with had been killed when a tree fell on his car (my aunt actually lives in this man's old house now). It really got them thinking about what their fate could have been.

My mammy thinks that the old lady may have been a ghost of an old woman who lived in a house, not far from where the tree fell. My maternal grandfather – who had just died fourteen months beforehand, was hired out to this house as a worker when he was a boy. He had always told my mother about an old woman who lived in the house. She was very kind to him and he always remembered her for that.

Was this my grandda's way of making sure my mammy and daddy were not to be forced apart that night by a terrible accident? I guess we'll never know for sure. One thing for sure is that mammy and daddy, to this day, cannot explain it logically.

I am a psychology graduate, and I spent a lot of time looking into near-death experiences. I don't think my professor was too pleased when I had to give a talk to my class on the topic. I think he was expecting me to come to the conclusion that it can all be explained by science – but it can't!

4

Family Ties

The stories in this chapter are generally testimonies relating to deceased family members who in many cases, make their presence felt when they are needed most, in particular at a significant or distressing time or at special moments such as a wedding, funeral or a moment of danger. These are mostly tales of reassurance.

John, Gloucestershire, England

As a small boy, my much loved brother died suddenly and I have spent the rest of my life trying to come to terms with that event. This was added to when my wife, Brenda, and I lost our eight year old son to leukaemia as well. The effects of these, and other happenings, have caused me to follow a fairly conventional, ecumenical Christian path. This continued until the time that my wife also succumbed to leukaemia.

For some months before her demise, I became increasingly aware of external interventions. Some would describe this as 'the hand of God guiding'. Since my wife had parted company with God soon after our son's death, and certainly when it became necessary for her to have a brain operation, partially to remove a brain tumour, she adamantly declared herself to be an atheist.

During the last three weeks, when her personal evolution concluded, I watched numerous mystical happenings. I have come to regard death as a stage in the evolutionary process when the spirit, or soul, no longer requires a body and sheds it, as the butterfly sheds its chrysalis, and as beautiful birds emerge from boring looking eggs.

For some months following her death, I was aware of signs, which could have been wishful thinking or trivial coincidence. That my wife, to whom I had been married for forty-eight years was still at hand was without doubt. I had brought to my attention, all manner of things, which were helpful and instructive in my efforts to look after myself. She knew my particular likes and loves and time and again, I had strong impulses, brought to my mind, which prompted me to do something, which had a bearing upon us both. I did not see visions nor did I hear ghostly rattlings. We always had a telepathic link. We had often laughed together, when one, or the other, would say words that the other had been forming in their heads.

It was obvious to me that she wished me to know that her essential person had survived death. Like the Easter story in which for a time Jesus made himself recognisable to his best friends, my wife Brenda kept saying 'I love you and I am with you always, even unto the end of the world'.

My most dramatic revelation was when I was in Ireland. I had never been there before. My friend and I went and returned through Rosslare, County Wexford and during our week's walks, we looked for B&Bs. The first farmhouse in which we stayed was the home of a man who had recently undergone a brain tumour operation. His wife and I had long discussions about what was involved in caring for one who was prone to epileptic fits and who needed to attend clinics regularly. They were devout Catholics but I had become a devout sceptic. As we left I patted each on their respective arms and wished them 'Christ be with you'. It seemed to be the right thing to do.

Having Scottish Highland origins and therefore Irish roots, as well as English, I am convinced that some of us have a natural endowment of second sight. I certainly admit to being a mystic and having a predisposition to matters psychic. There were other meetings and conversations of surprising subjective significance. The final exciting climax came when driving through county Wicklow, along a small coastal road, near Brittas Bay. I came to a spot large enough for two or three cars to park. Having always loved being near the sea, we stopped and I got out to walk along the beach, which strongly reminded me of one I had known since a child. My companion opted to stay in the car because it was 'too cold', which is interesting because 'ghostly' manifestations are often accompanied by feelings of considerable coldness. I walked down by the water and recalled similar walks by the sea with my brother, my son, my parents and my wife. As their mental images came into my mind, their spiritual presences became evident to me. It was a calm day, yet there was a rushing of wind and I was aware of the spiritual presence of each of them for some brief time. The arrival of one of them was accompanied by a deliberate nudge, so that I could have no doubt that they were there. I strolled with them for no more than a minute, if that, with tears of happiness welling up in my eyes. I returned to the car but said nothing to my companion.

The response of those to whom I recount these details varies. My surviving son, at first, was convinced that my mind had been turned by bereavement. Some others looked sceptical, never having had similar reasons to contemplate the full meaning of life and death. However others know all about it because they too have had their own experiences and understand that death is not the end of life. Indeed eternal life is precisely that, and those who have formed deep loving attachments in life are still able to communicate with those who have moved just a little breath away.

John, County Dublin, Ireland

I work with early school leavers, and this involves getting to know them personally. In return they also get to know me. One of the youngsters I discovered loved poetry and we often sat and talked about Patrick Kavanagh, Yeats and Wordsworth, as well as sharing our own attempts at writing poetry.

During a recent presentation of certificates to the youth I noticed a lady standing to the side observing me throughout the ceremony. She waited behind until the group was leaving and took me aside saying, 'Since I've heard about you I've wanted to thank you'.

I then discovered that she was the mother of the young girl who loved poetry and wanted to express her admiration for the work our group does. She then added, 'The best way I know how to thank you is to tell you about your father who wants me to pass on a message and to beg you for your forgiveness.' (I had fallen out with my father before he died and I now firmly believe this was his way of returning to apologise.) The lady spoke of my father's wishes for her to warn me about 'the wiring you've had done in the recent extension of your house. Have it checked!'

As you can imagine, I was taken aback. The lady continued, 'To prove your father's observations he said he has noticed that a houseplant was recently moved from inside the house to the back wall of your garden'. In life, my father loved gardening and houseplants.

I returned home to my wife a little bewildered and somewhat spooked. My wife was even more so when I disclosed the information to her, and she confirmed that she had taken a houseplant down to the back wall of the garden the previous day.

We immediately had an electrician in to survey the wiring in the extension and were horrified to hear of his findings. An earth wire had been left disconnected in one light socket, where the wire had been cut too short and was left hanging, posing a threat of electrocution. A second fault was found in another light socket where water had managed to get in, and thirdly the new bathroom that was built as part of the new extension was found to have a dangerous electric shower. The electrician discovered there were no screws holding the plastic covering over the main wire system of the shower. I later learned it had almost come off completely whilst one of my daughters was showering. This could have resulted in a very serious accident.

The electrician agreed that my father's message from beyond the grave was certainly uncanny but had definitely saved a life through his advice to have our wiring checked.

There was always stress and tension between my father and me. Needless to say, I have forgiven my father and now possess a deep sense of gratitude for his care, especially for the grandchildren he never had the opportunity to know in life, as they were born after his death.

Lee, Glasgow, Scotland

I remember her face like it was yesterday. As I walked up the aisle on my wedding day, I caught sight of my great-granny sitting in her wheelchair just left of the church pulpit. She looked fabulous – colour co-ordinated outfit, bright sparkling blue eyes and a smile that told a thousand stories. A series of strokes had robbed her of her speech, but granny had no need for words that day.

I was so pleased she'd made it, as I had long feared illness or age would take her from us before the big day. However, at the age of ninety-one she had done me proud and sat beaming beside my grandparents.

Despite it being the 'best day of my life', I had a prevailing sense of sadness. The relationship had been rocky and I felt I was on a roller coaster, one from which I could not alight. The smiles on the day hid a thousand doubts about my new husband, whose urge to control me and my every move had tainted our short engagement.

However, I kept up the pretence, the whole wedding was too huge not to. Little did I know at the time, but my whole family shared my sadness and doubt.

Once back from our honeymoon, I resolved to make the most of married life. Things settled down into a rather mundane routine and the nagging sadness in my heart would not go away.

Four months after the wedding, I received a phone call to say that my great-granny had died. Twenty-fourth December 1999. This date is now etched on my memory for something other than the exchanging of gifts and merriment.

Before the funeral, I was consumed by a feeling of guilt and sadness. Sadness that she'd gone but joy that the last time she saw me she believed I was happy and settled. I was given a photo of granny with us on our wedding day and, after she died, I put it on our mantelpiece to remind me of her special smile.

One day, when alone in the house, I remember picking the photo up and saying aloud: 'Sorry granny, the last time you saw me you thought I was happy – sorry for lying – if you can hear me you'll know what's in my heart.'

That night I lay awake for hours, just thinking. Once asleep, though, I had the strangest dream. My great-granny popped into my dream momentarily and said, 'Don't be daft lassie – get that picture off the mantelpiece – I don't want to be up there on show!'

I laughed about it the next day and left the photo where it was. That's when things started happening. The following evening we were sound asleep when a loud commotion erupted around 4a.m., much like a raucous party outside our bedroom window.

We jumped out of bed to investigate and discovered the noise was coming from the living-room, some way along the hall. I was terrified – what if someone had broken in? Any burglar capable of making such a noise must have been mad, I reasoned.

We tiptoed along to the living-room door – armed with golf clubs. As we flung the door open, I was stunned to see the television on and the volume turned up full. What amazed me the most was that I always turned it off overnight, rather than leave it on stand-by, as part of my own personal energy saving crusade!

As a believer, I was convinced it was a sign of sorts, but my husband shirked it off as one of those things. The following day, he went out and I was left alone for a few hours. Still intrigued by what had happened the night before, I was wandering silently along the hall when a photo fell out of its frame on the wall and slid onto the floor in front of me.

I smiled and said, 'Ok, granny, I'll move your picture and put it up there instead of this one.' I took it from the mantelpiece and placed it in the hall – and she must have been happy because things calmed down for a while.

Unfortunately, things did not calm down in the marriage. My husband's controlling streak took over and he chipped away at my self-esteem daily, slating my appearance, my job, my ambitions, my family and friends. Determined to make a go of the marriage, despite his behaviour, I kept going but I threatened to leave him more than once, on one occasion I even had my bags packed, but his histrionics persuaded me to stay. He was clever that way.

We moved back down beside my family, and I gradually started to draw strength from their love and support. He, on the other hand, simply became nastier. One Saturday night, while he was up on his computer in an internet chat room, I sat alone downstairs with a glass of wine. Listening to my favourite music, I sat crossed-legged on the floor and sobbed. I knew the marriage was over, had known for some time, but I had no idea how to get out of it.

Suddenly the living-room door opened and the temperature dropped. I was aware of a distinctive odour, much like a cross between earth, damp and soft perfume.

My great-granny was back.

I stared at the open door and smiled through my tears, 'I know that's you granny, thanks for coming back.' At that point I felt calm for the first time in months. The permanent knot in my stomach was easing and I remember feeling a sense of clarity in my head – I had to get out of this marriage.

I did not share my thoughts with my husband. Instead I kept them close to my heart.

In October 2001, we split up. It was messy, protracted

and hostile but I had managed to get out of the very relationship that was killing my spirit, and it felt good.

After the separation, I slowly started to get my life back on track. However, thoughts of my great-granny were never far away and I had the overwhelming urge to try and speak to her myself – to thank her for her help.

I sensed her with me. She opened her heart to me for over an hour. She said I had a very strong soul, while my ex's was very weak, and I had done the right thing coming out of the marriage. She said I should not worry about letting her down, that she was very proud of me and would stay with me for a few years to make sure I was on the right track.

I asked if she had turned on the television, pushed the photo out of its frame and opened my door that evening, and she said she had done so to get my attention.

There were other things that she said about my ex that hit home too. The way he stared menacingly at me when he was angry, his controlling, devious nature and the way he always managed to leave me without a penny while he had a wallet full of notes. It was all so accurate, as if she had been living there with us.

Now, I am far more aware of the presence of my great-granny – and perhaps other spirits too. Periodically, I smell the distinctive odour I now recognise as the scent of the spirits. I'm also aware of cold spots, when they're around me, and am not afraid to ask for help if needs be. Usually, after an impromptu chat with my spirit friends, the stomach knots go and the mental clarity returns, like a spiritual hug!

Coincidence? The onset of madness? Strong yearning to believe? Who knows?

I do.

Celine, County Kilkenny, Ireland

My name is Celine and I'm thirty-five years of age and married with two children. When I was eleven years of age my nine-year-old brother Phelim died in a tragic accident. The pain was unbearable and I still miss him today.

Many years later whilst living in my first house with my husband and toddler, I had some strange experiences which at the time terrified me. The first related to a bag of clothes pegs of all things! I had bought some and was looking for them one day. I searched the kitchen and was getting very frustrated so asked Phelim to help me. I then forgot about it and went upstairs but when I came down about thirty minutes later, the pegs were sitting on the shelf in full view. I had removed everything from that shelf during my search and they definitely weren't there when I went upstairs and there was just me and my child, who was upstairs with me, in the house.

Around the same time my husband was working away and I was suffering from anxiety. I missed him so much and used to cry a lot. During the worst time when I was sobbing I always got a smell of aftershave around me. I know it was Phelim and felt better immediately.

Also, when my son was about three (he's seven now), we were staying in my parent's house and he was in bed in Phelim's old room. He called me and said he couldn't sleep because he was scared of 'him'. I asked who, he said 'him', and pointed at the wall. There was obviously nothing there that I could see but it did made me wonder. Did Phelim visit my son that night? I'll never know, but I like to think he did.

John, County Mayo, Ireland

As a child I remember an old grandfather clock in the house where my uncle lived. It was there long before I was born, its chimes and slow tick-tock always fascinated me. Then one day out of the blue the striking mechanism developed a problem and the churning stopped. Regardless of this it continued to tick away, still keeping correct time, but so keen was my uncle to get it back in working order that he spent much of his spare time trying to have it ringing and working again but all his efforts were in vain. The clock was never to strike again.

After my uncle died the grandfather clock was moved to my elder brother's home. Later they removed the weights and pendulums which put an end to the clock as a time keeper.

Some time later my younger brother and I were visiting our brother and were invited to stay overnight and shared the spare bedroom, the very place where the grandfather clock now stood, ever silent, in the corner.

We chatted far into the night and much of the conversation was about our uncle and his obsession with the clock all those years ago. At last we decided to put the lights out and go to sleep. The now dark and silent room was the perfect atmosphere for our tired and weary bones. Everything was quiet as we awaited the moment when we would drop off to sleep.

Then suddenly we were aroused as the grandfather clock in the corner came to life. We could hear distinctly, as we listened, with shock and amazement, that whirring sound and the sharp click which was so familiar to our ears all those years ago, when our uncle tried desperately to get the old clock to strike.

Our immediate reaction was to switch on the light and find out if it were possible for the clock's mechanism to work in such a manner without the aid of its weights or pendulum. This became clear, as we carried out a thorough examination, that without such essentials as weights and pendulums there wasn't the slightest possibility that any movement of the clock mechanism could occur.

There may be a scientific answer to all of this but until that answer comes the strange happenings of eight years ago will always be a mystery to my brother and I.

I sometimes ask myself this question: 'Did the spirit of our dead uncle pay us a visit that night just to try one more time to have his beloved grandfather clock strike the hour again?'

Only very recently I came upon the old clock again. It now stands in the corner of my brother's outhouse. I gazed at it for a while, almost expecting it to react but it was silent, its former grandeur now gone with a section of once beautiful woodwork missing. It looked a sad sight indeed.

Edward, County Dublin, Ireland

My wife Mary and I and our dearly beloved daughter Maureen shared a love that I can only describe as unique; unique because of the many, many thousands of married couples who for various reasons have separated and even divorced – and those that are still together speak of their partners in less than glowing terms and even sometimes stay together only for the sake of the children. Mary and Maureen had a relationship that was almost out of this world. After thirty-two years of such a happy marriage, Mary died – Maureen had died in 1985 – and almost every day from the day I was left on my own I've asked them if they would, if able, show themselves to me in their present state.

What happened on Saturday 17 April 2004 I believe was in reply to my request. I'd arrived home after Mass and was thinking of the kind lady who'd given me the usual lift home, when without warning and with the speed of light I was conscious of having been transported – not physically but spiritually – because none of my senses were working. I had no sense of smell, touch or hearing but my eyes seemed to be covered in something through which I could only see a kind of blue – a light brown blue and nothing more. I recall thinking I must be somewhere in a time before Mary and Maureen died because I couldn't be this happy otherwise; as the happiness began to build and strengthen – I wondered how I was so happy.

I began to feel a love being directed at me from all directions. How I could tell it was love I don't know, only that it came from hundreds of thousands of what can only be souls and from every point on the compass, as though I were at the centre of a globe. When the happiness and love had reached immense proportions I – quickly as sight – was back to normality with no after effects at all, but the memory was vivid and real and as sharp then as it is today.

The whole experience lasted perhaps five or six seconds, although it could have been longer since I believe it happened in a different time zone and on a different plane.

One thing I'm certain of is that it was real and it did take place – where, I've no idea, but it was only my mind or soul that went because all of my senses were left behind.

I feel that Mary and Maureen lifted a corner to give me a brief peek at the life they are now enjoying. They couldn't show themselves to me but perhaps they did what they could in reply to my continual requests. I do know that during their lives here on earth we couldn't do enough for each other and the happiness we enjoyed was unbelievable.

In my prayers every night I thank dear Jesus for giving us all such a wonderfully happy and carefree time together.

Paul, Nottingham, England

My father died of cancer on New Year's Day 1991. At the time I was fourteen years old. Nine years later I had moved to another city and met my wife-to-be Caroline. She had two sons already. About a year into the relationship Caroline fell pregnant and we ended up moving to a new house. Three months later our son Colin was born.

One night Caroline had taken Colin upstairs to settle

him down for the night and I switched the baby monitor on. Caroline came back downstairs into the front room. We sat down and started to play on the playstation. After about ten minutes I heard the voice of a man over the baby monitor saying 'Ah, isn't he cute?'

Becoming alarmed, I ran upstairs and checked his room. The room was really cold when I entered. I checked the whole house. With Caroline's help we checked the doors. Everywhere was locked up. My other two sons were fast asleep so Caroline decided to go to bed. She went upstairs and I made a hot drink and followed her up. I put Caroline's drink on her side of the bed and mine on my side.

After a few minutes Caroline went to take a drink of the coffee and complained that it was stone cold. Thinking I had forgotten to boil the kettle Caroline went out of the bedroom. As soon as she stepped out of the room the coffee was red hot. She walked back into the room and the coffee was stone cold. This made us both very nervous.

We both went onto the top of the stairs to have a cigarette. About five minutes later Caroline nudged me and said 'look down at the bottom of the stairs.' I looked down and couldn't believe what I saw. There was my dad! He smiled, gave me the thumbs up and disappeared.

Caroline had never seen a picture of my dad as I had lost contact with my family but she described him to a tee. There is no way she could have known as I had not mentioned him to her. We didn't sleep with the light off that night. I felt peaceful but Caroline was frightened.

I got the impression my dad approved of my son Colin – his grandchild.

Sonia, Jersey, Channel Islands

After my mother died my sister and I were sorting out her little treasures and we remarked that her room, which had been shut up for a few days, smelt very stale and musty. When we had finished our sad task I looked up, vaguely heavenwards and said aloud 'Mother dear, I hope we are handling things as you would have wished.' Immediately the most beautiful perfume filled the room and my sister and I looked at each other in amazement, having absolutely no idea where it could have come from as we were not wearing perfume and there were no flowers in or near the room. As children we had often told mother that she smelt lovely. She was fond of good perfume and we felt that day that she had managed to express her approval of what we were doing. After a minute or two the scent faded, never to return.

The second incident refers to my late husband. He had been ill for a long time but had always remembered where he had put things and when I, or the friend who helped me nurse him, needed a hammer or maybe some wiring or whatever, he would point us in the right direction and sure enough it would be there. He would then laugh and say 'When I am gone you women will not be able to find anything!' He died just over thirteen years ago and every so often I believe he hides things. Although I am a tidy and methodical person I often find I have to search the house for some little thing I am sure should be in its appointed place and is not. Finally I say aloud 'William darling, stop messing about and let me find it.' And of course I do. It is lovely to feel his mischievous spirit is not far away!

Judy, New South Wales, Australia

On 13 May 1998 my husband and I were staying at a small wooden holiday cottage on New Zealand's South Island, which is approximately a three-and-a-half-hour flight from Sydney, Australia, where we live. We were half-way through a two-week holiday. At approximately 5 p.m. on that day I was in the lounge/dining area of the cottage and my husband Harry was outside cleaning the car we had hired. I looked up at the overhead beam of the open doorway to the adjoining room and saw a photo image of my mother in an old-style oval frame and next to that was a silver pewter-type moulded image of a man's face in profile – similar to that used often in children's books to represent the face of the sun or moon. My mother's image was of her about fifteen years younger than her then age of eighty-eight.

These apparitions were so clear that I went to my husband and told him, as I had never experienced anything like this before and felt I should let someone know so that I could be believed later if necessary. As it turned out, my mother (who had been in a nursing home in Sydney for nearly four years) had died about seven hours earlier that day – a fact we did not learn until four days later as we could not be contacted by family until we were in a more accessible location.

When our elder daughter got in touch by phone I was able to pin-point the day of my mother's death before I was told. My younger daughter said later, 'It took Nana nearly the whole day to find you!' This she said rather tongue-in-cheek as she knew the tenacious nature of the woman.

Caroline, County Wexford, Ireland

My mother died in the room opposite my bedroom on 21 January 2002 at 10.40 p.m. She was gone out of our house by 1 a.m. and I know her spirit was in our house afterwards. How I know is because I was awoken from a deep sleep at 5 a.m. to hear my mother speaking into my ear. I saw nothing but the room was very still – my husband also woke and I didn't say anything about the incident to him as he'd say I was crazy. She said 'Everything went well. I'm happy now. Pray for me and I'll pray for you and I'll always be looking down on you.'

I have great faith. I visit my mother and father's grave once a week and I sometimes sense their presence in the chapel as I pray. I'm not afraid of death at all.

Patricia, Delaware, USA

My husband died from cancer. We were married fifty-four years. He liked to remind me that we were joined together like the legs of a clothes pin and our special song was *Side by Side*.

Watching him suffer from that terrible disease for five years was heart-wrenching. He died a virtual skeleton and left me without him, feeling alone and lost.

I could not cry, my throat was swollen shut. In my heart

93

I felt I had cried enough silent tears to last an eternity.

A week after the funeral my son Paul drove me to our lawyer's to sign more papers concerning my husband. My heart was still so heavy I thought I couldn't bear this emptiness much longer.

Upon returning home I slumped down in my chair ready to just remain there and drift into an accepted nothing.

My son gently touched my arm and said, 'Mom, there's a message left on your cell phone, the light is red.'

'You take it,' I said, 'I do not want to talk with anyone.'

Paul opened the phone and his face was ashen. He handed the phone to me. There was a text message which read, 'I will always love you. I am OK.' What a cruel joke I thought and handed the phone back to my son.

There was the telephone number from the sender at the top of the text message. Paul angrily called it. 'Did you just text my mother?' he asked.

The answer was in broken English. 'I no know your mother! I no know how to text!'

After Paul told me of the man's response to his angry question I was stunned. Then an unbelievable warmth spread through me and I sobbed tears for a forever lifetime and a forever love.

5

Messengers from Beyond

The most celebrated apparition of a person who died is that of Jesus Christ. Following his public execution and burial, many of his followers, both women and men, testified publicly that he had appeared to them in various locations. Thereafter their lives were characterised by a newfound confidence and hope that marked them as people without fear.

The works of William Shakespeare and Charles Dickens feature famous ghosts who appear as messengers of conscience and moral challenge. In Roman Catholicism there are testimonies of Marian and saintly apparitions.

Here, several people tell their stories of apparitions of deceased loved ones, friends and, sometimes, unwelcome strangers. If what they say is to be believed, it appears that the dead are not dead and exist in another realm and form. Some have the ability to manifest themselves in a visual and often familiar way. Often, it seems, their appearance is experienced as a comfort, reassurance or protection.

John, County Cork, Ireland

It was five minutes to midnight when I left my friend's home in County Cork. It was the early 1960s and I was in my teens. I crossed the main Cork/Dublin road and moved onto what was known locally as the 'black boreen'. The name was given to it because according to tradition a black man guarded a coffin of gold buried there. It was also claimed, if somebody should dig it up, a relative of that family would die prematurely.

The gateway entrance to my parent's farmhouse laneway fronts this boreen, so I slipped in there and set about closing the double gate. While doing so I heard a piercing wail coming from the direction of some nearby terraced houses. The wail shocked me but I proceeded down the laneway toward the farmhouse.

I slipped into the living-room. My parents and two brothers were already in bed so I sneaked quietly upstairs but on the landing my mother's voice filled the air. 'You're late again. Go into bed and no talk out of you.'

'I heard a wail coming from a house in the terrace,' I replied.

'Somebody was trying to frighten you,' came the reply.

It was time to retire to bed so I went into the room where my two brothers were sleeping in opposite beds. I told them about my experience. 'Oh, it was the banshee,' my elder brother said, 'a supernatural wail associated with some families before an impending death.' I got into bed beside him and relaxed as best I knew how. Finally I dozed off to sleep.

Next morning the milking of cows was the first task to be taken on. Three of us were milking by hand which was the norm at this time. Meanwhile some customers living in the terraced houses bought milk from us on a daily basis. Suddenly a young man appeared at the cow-house doorway, a milk container in his hand. My mother came from the dwelling house. A pint of measure hung from a large milk container outside. 'Can I have four pints of milk this morning?' It asked the young man standing outside.

'Certainly Dinny,' mother replied and she proceeded to pour that amount into the container in his hand.

'My mother died last night at midnight,' he said.

'Oh! I'm sorry. She was so gentle,' my mother said.

Then the dead woman's son took off in silence and headed homewards.

'So, that's where that wail came from last night,' I said. 'The banshee came for that poor woman.'

'It haunts some families,' my mother remarked. My father didn't join in because he didn't believe in it.

Five years passed. I was polishing and shining my shoes in the living-room of the farmhouse. According to the wall clock, it was almost two in the afternoon. My mother came down the stairs and frowned at me. 'Go out and help your father to feed the animals for the night. Those shoes can wait,' she said.

'Right mother,' I muttered. All of a sudden I went into shock. I almost clung to the chair I was sitting on. I began to perspire, but I stood up, dumped the shoes in a remote corner and went out.

Once I was in the fresh air I recovered quickly but I

couldn't figure out what had caused it. Later that evening the postman appeared in the yard. I was heading out and he handed me a small green envelope – a telegram that people always dreaded back along the years. I hurried back into the farmhouse and gave it to my mother. She slit the light green envelope open and read it aloud: *William O'Connell Died (stop) at 2 p.m. (stop) Signed Batt (stop)*. She dropped the telegram on the living-room table. I told her about the shock that came over me at 2 p.m. while I was shining my shoes. The bad news saddened her because William was her brother. Then she burst out crying.

Charlotte, Cumbria, England

When I married my husband we lived in a rented flat that was known to have a history of ghostly occurrences. The couple who had lived there before us fled one day and never came back. Undeterred we took the flat and proceeded to renovate it to our taste. This took us many months to do, during which time tools and other objects were moved. We would leave things deliberately in certain places and when we went back the next day they were always in a different place, despite no one having access. My husband thought it was me playing tricks.

We had been married just three days when I was woken in the night by a pressure on my legs. I sat up in bed and to my horror, saw an old man sitting on the bed just staring at me. He was dressed in the uniform of a soldier of the First World War and was dishevelled and dirty but the look of malevolence on his face was unforgettable! He was horrible and I knew instinctively that he was not a benign spirit. I tried to scream but could only manage to make a sound in my throat. My husband woke up and shook me and was very shocked when he saw how distressed I was. I told him about the soldier but not about the way he was dressed, as I was upset and did not want to talk about it. He humoured me but I could tell he did not believe me. He said that he did not believe in ghosts.

Some weeks later the marriage was in trouble. We argued all the time and the flat was always cold, no matter how much heating we had on. It was a very dark and depressing atmosphere and things were still happening.

One day I made a joke about the soldier and I was leaning out of the kitchen window at the time. A few days later my husband was very agitated and would not speak to me. I persisted in asking him what was wrong and he told me had seen the soldier too! He accurately described what he was wearing and also the sense of evil he felt. He was very shaken and did not want to upset me by sharing his experience. We moved house soon after that and everything was fine. My husband now tells all sceptics about his experience and says he will never doubt again.

Paul, County Wicklow, Ireland

My wife and I experienced a strange incident in Wexford in October 1975. It happened as we were driving home to Dublin, where I was living at the time, late at night. After making our way around some bends on the road between Ennis-corthy and Gorey, we came to a straight section and in the distance I saw a car approaching, with the headlights on full. As the two cars got closer I dipped my lights but the other driver did not. I continued driving and at the very point at which the two cars passed each other, a young man, about twenty-three to twenty-six years old, ran across the bonnet of my car. I jammed on the brakes in order to avoid hitting him. The other car did not stop. My wife then got out to see if the young man was all right but he was nowhere to be found. Even though I was travelling at about thirty-five miles per hour, it was not possible for me to have missed him. I reversed the car in order to help search using my lights, without any luck. My wife got back into the car and after talking about what had just happened, we realised there was no way we could have missed him. The fact that we did not see his legs as he moved across the car gave us a very uneasy feeling about the incident. We talked about him all the way home.

As we discussed this whole situation we both agreed we did not see his legs as he was quite literally moving across the front of the car. We sat up all night writing down the details of what we had witnessed. We both described exactly the same young man, age and style of clothes – tweed jacket, and a deerstalker hat. To this day we wonder what really happened that night.

6

Thank You for the Music

One of the co-authors of this book had musical coincidences in life related to a best friend who died tragically in 1976. In all cases the coincidences were so specific and poignant that he sensed, at a deeper level, it was his friend's way of letting him know that he was still close, though in a different dimension.

The coincidences related to songs with relevance to both our lives. Each occurred at a highly significant moment that not only caused him to remember but to actually sense his presence.

The contributors to this chapter record similar experiences.

Jerica, Washington, USA

The following is my story of what happened when my dad passed away. Born nearly three months early in May of 1949, to Irish parents, I was adopted at the age of ten days by a couple who were considered too old to adopt by traditional adoption agencies. My father's cousin was a nurse at the hospital where I was born and when she found out I was to be put up for adoption she immediately called my dad and said, 'We have a premature baby who will be up for adoption. If you come right away, you can put in for the adoption without an agency being involved. I think it's a boy.'

She was in such a hurry to contact my dad she didn't know I was a girl! My parents-to-be met me, fell in love and took me home on Mother's Day! As a premature baby all I wanted to do was sleep, and it was my dad's job to wake me up by pinching me! Dad said he would hold me right in the palm of his hand. He would hold me while sitting in the rocking-chair, pinch me, feed me, and soothe me with his deep vibrato voice by singing to me. That was the start of an incredible bond for this daddy's girl.

Throughout my life there were two songs that were our favourite. One was *You are My Sunshine*, and the second was *With Someone Like You*.

Fast forward to the year 2000. My mother battled breast cancer, then lymphoma for more than five years, and lost the struggle in June of 2000. My dad was ninety-two years old at that time. They had been married fifty-three years. My mom was of Scotch/Irish descent and we were often told how much we looked alike.

My dad was second-generation Norwegian. We used to joke about how the Vikings were always raiding Ireland and taking the best women!

Dad moved from his retirement community in California up to my home in Washington. He had spent most of his life in Washington working in public relations for a major bank so he had a number of friends and family here.

He ultimately had to give up driving, one of his favourite

activities, and that was the beginning of the end. He just kind of gave up, and just short of his ninety-fifth birthday he passed away.

I was devastated! It was hard when mom passed away, but I had to be strong for dad, so I never really let myself grieve. When dad died everything just overwhelmed me. As an only child I had dealt with so much over the previous five years! He passed away early in the morning and it wasn't until early evening, after settling things with the funeral home, that I was able to return home with my husband. It was then that it all really hit me. I went into our bedroom and let go. All day one of the songs we used to sing kept going through my head. I tried to sing it, but just couldn't do it. I cried so long and hard that my head was splitting. I tried to go to sleep, but was too agitated. I decided to watch some television.

Our living-room has two chairs facing the television with a hanging lamp between the two chairs. This lamp has no switch, but is turned on by my touching the metal at the top of the shade. The light reflects in the television so we never turn it on while watching television.

I turned on the television and a movie was in progress, it was *Out of Africa* with Meryl Streep and Robert Redford. I always loved that movie, but was only paying slight attention. My husband was sitting at his desk in the next room.

I was only sitting there a few minutes when suddenly the hanging lamp illuminated, and simultaneously the song *With Someone Like You* was coming from the television! I started to sing along with the music and was filled with a strong sense of peace. When the song ended, my husband called to me, 'I can't believe that song was just on the television!'

I said, 'Yeah, well if you can't believe that you'll never believe this! The light turned on all by itself at the same time!'

Since then we have rearranged furniture and have moved that lamp to another location. It has mysteriously lit up a couple of more times. The most recent was on Christmas Eve last. We were totally delighted and at the same time my husband and I said, 'Hi dad! Merry Christmas!'

Paul, Shrewsbury, England

My late father-in-law Eric was not a believer in any type of afterlife. I had spoken to him of my beliefs but being a very down to earth and practical man, he could not accept any possibilities of a continued existence.

This prevailed even after the loss of his wife, several years before his own demise. Eric died after a two-week illness, in intensive care, a few years ago. During his life, my wife Joy had mentioned that the song *Danny Boy* had been his favourite and that he had often sung along to it.

Uncannily, we began to experience, for two years, that whenever a tape featuring *Danny Boy* was played in our home that tape would stop, even when the tape was a compilation album.

The next happening is the most interesting. Approximately two years after his death, Joy and I had just sat down in a pub for a lunch on a Saturday afternoon. Joy placed her brand new mobile phone on the table. I visited the gent's toilet and came back to be accused by my wife of messing about. When I asked what she meant she said that the mobile had rang and she had answered, only to hear strained breathing. She paled when she showed me the number of the caller. It was my late father-in-law's exact number, without the STD code. I ran out of the pub with the mobile in my hand, with the intention of redialling this number.

We had sold Eric's house a few months after his death. We had never even met the new owners and they could have no way of knowing my wife's new phone number. I tried several times to redial the number, each time getting the no number tone. To this day I believe that my father-in-law had chosen the mobile as a last means of contact – possibly to signal to my wife that he was now moving on from being around her.

We have never had any happenings since.

Sandra, Bristol, England

My father was from Ireland and had a beautiful tenor singing voice. He was always singing around the house, sometimes happy songs, sometimes sad depending on his mood. However, for as long as I could remember, every time he sang *The Mountains of Mourne*, I would begin to cry, not sobbing crying, just quietly swallowing back the tears and feeling an overwhelming sense of loss.

At sixty years of age, my father contracted cancer and was hospitalised overnight in order to have a blood transfusion. The next morning, the weather was very grey and overcast with heavy black clouds as far as the eye could see. I was alone in my flat and looking out at the weather deciding whether to go out or not when on the radio came this male voice singing *The Mountains of Mourne*. As I listened, the clouds began to part and a shaft of sunlight pierced the gloom. As the song ended the clouds closed up again and I knew that my father had died. The realisation of why I had always cried when I heard that song became apparent. It was his swan song and his way of telling me that life goes on after death. A few minutes later, the phone rang. It was the hospital and with tears streaming down my face, I heard the voice on the other end of the phone tell me that my father had died. 'I know,' I said, 'I know'.

Jean, Forfarshire, Scotland

Many years ago I was arranging our Golden Charter when I asked my husband George what hymns he would like sung at his funeral. 'Ack, never mind, just sing *Once in a While*,' he said. George always got up before me to shower, shave, etc. then he would go into the kitchen and put on the radio for the news. Terry Wogan was on the *Pause for Thought* – that's when I used to join him for a cup of tea.

On 12 February 2003, I came into the kitchen. George suddenly grabbed the worktop. I asked if he was dizzy again. He could not answer and slipped slowly to the floor. I could hardly get down to him as I had a plaster on my broken leg. However I did hold his hand and spoke to him: 'Don't leave me, I need you.' It was too late. He rolled his eyes to me and gurgled something. Then he was gone. He was eighty-three years of age. I asked our past president to sing his song at the lovely service she gave.

A year went by and on the 12 February I came into the kitchen and put on Radio 1. *Pause for Thought* was presented by a lady and when she finished the music started. I was standing where George fell so I had to sit down and listen. When it finished Terry Wogan said, 'That was Johnny Mathis singing *Once in a While*.'

It was magic to me. George was saying 'I'm all right now.' I'll never forget it. *Once in a While* is a song you don't hear that often.

Michael, County Cork, Ireland

My father died suddenly on 13 January 2002 at the age of fifty-eight. My first inexplicable experience occurred shortly afterwards.

After returning to my car one lunchtime during which I was thinking of my dad and wondering was there any way he could contact me, communicate with me or give me some sign that he still existed somewhere – I turned on the radio to hear a particular song end, and the DJ Ronan Collins tell his audience that what was just heard was *A Message to Michael* sung by Dionne Warwick. I got an immediate jolt and sat stunned wondering whether I was hearing things. As if sensing my disbelief the DJ reiterated the name of the song. I pulled over the car and was satisfied that I had received a particular sign. The fact that these were the first words I heard

107

when I turned on the radio, the words themselves having a particular meaning to me and the incident occurring at a time when I was searching for a sign, confirmed to me that there is another level at work somewhere.

Carol, Guernsey, Channel Islands

In August 2003 my twenty-nine-year-old daughter died suddenly whilst we were away on holiday in England. I had a very close bond with her.

The night she died I had a strange dream. A veiled face came towards me and kissed me, making me giggle. I could not see whose face it was, but I felt that I knew them. Strangely, my daughter's closest friend also had the same dream that night. We received the news of her death the next day.

This began a train of strange happenings. We had to choose music for the funeral service. The family chose two songs and, with her best friend, we were looking for a third piece of music. The friend suggested *Somewhere over the Rainbow* by Eva Cassidy, which she knew my daughter liked as she had recently played it to her. As the suggestion was made all three of us felt icy cold and there was a definite presence with us.

Following the funeral, my husband and I visited Jersey for a weekend. At lunchtime we went into a favourite cafe for our lunch. Being out of season we were the only customers and we sat in the quiet dining area, ordered our food and as we sat chatting we were suddenly aware of the Eva Cassidy song playing. We were both sure that no music was playing as we entered and ordered our food. I was so overcome with emotion I had to leave the restaurant until the song had finished. We have heard the other songs from the funeral at special moments since, but never this song in the same way.

7

All Creatures Great and Small

The incidences related in this chapter focus on the link between humankind and nature. Places of scenic beauty, or a much loved pet or creature, significant to the deceased and bereaved, are central to the stories which, once again, emphasise that death may not be the end.

Ray, Carmarthenshire, Wales

I am a member of the Baha'i faith and thought it might be interesting to obtain stories about death from another culture/ religion.

My wife Lynda had been diagnosed with cancer, and had gradually declined in health for five years, as the cancer spread. I had given up work to care for her and during that time at home I spent my spare time reading and investigating various aspects of life. It was during this time I discovered the Baha'i faith.

Like any adherent to a religion, I obviously wanted to share my belief with those I loved.

However, in Lynda I met resistance. She had no real belief and in view of her frail health I did not pursue the subject.

To clarify the story I must explain a little about the Baha'i faith. We believe that God has sent a series of messengers over the centuries, and these include Abraham, Moses, Christ, Muhammad, Krishna and Baha'u'llah. Each has a message that relates to the time they come to earth, so all religions are really one. We also believe that when we die our soul is free and continues to a new plane of existence. We cannot understand fully what this next plane has in store as it is just beyond our understanding. We use a simple parable to explain this – a plant lives but has no knowledge of the life that an animal enjoys, an animal has knowledge of plants but has no understanding about the complexity of man and will relate to man in the same way it would another animal, and will have not the slightest idea of all we can do and understand. So man understand the plants and the animals but cannot understand the next plane (and tries to explain it using terms that we understand).

It was the last night of my wife's earthly life and she was in a hospice where she had gone the day before at her own request. It was the middle of the night and I was sitting alone with her. She was pretty drugged up and unconscious most of the time. The first time she awoke during the night she was quite rational and asked me what I thought happened when we die. I knew she was not in a fit state for a theological discussion so I used a simple story to try and explain the concept of what I believed. I told her that as a caterpillar comes to the end of its life and approaches its death it has no knowledge of being a butterfly. However, when it dies it becomes

111

this beautiful creature and soars high, losing the shackles that had caused it to remain earthbound, so at the time of our death we become something wonderful like the butterfly. At this stage she fell asleep again, and I thought that was the end of the matter.

Later in the night she awoke for the second, and final, time. This awakening was very brief and all she said was 'I like the idea of being a butterfly'. This obviously gave me some comfort and I wondered if perhaps she had found God in that semi-conscious state. I would never know.

Since Lynda had no religious affiliations and I was a strong Baha'i I decided that her funeral would be on Baha'i lines and I would lead the ceremony myself, with the help of friends who would read from all the great holy books. As part of this ceremony I told the story of Lynda's last night, and the butterfly story.

As people were leaving, one of my Baha'i friends, who also knew Lynda came up to me in tears and said she had something wonderful to tell me, but she was too emotional to tell me now and would send her husband with a letter later that day.

This woman was a rational and intelligent woman whom I respected for her level-headedness, so I was curious what this letter might contain. When the letter arrived it explained how on the morning of the funeral a butterfly had come into the house and fluttered around. My friend didn't want to harm the butterfly and was concerned that in February it was too early for it to be around so she called her husband.

He said 'wait for it to settle' and then he would take it out-side into the sun. They waited and watched and the butterfly eventually settled on a photo of Baha'u'llah (the founder of our religion). My friend was convinced that this was Lynda telling me that after our butterfly conversation she had in-deed found God and was comforting me. My friend had not heard the butterfly story until the ceremony and was visibly shaken so I believe what she told me about the incident. It gave me some comfort but it was just one incident and could have been a coincidence so whilst I remembered it, I put the matter away. Some weeks later I was visiting a friend in Chicago and there were floods which caused the plumbing of the house to back up. My friend was very embarrassed and offered to pay for me to go stay in a hotel. I said no, I would go and tour a little and then return in a week or so when the situation was resolved. I don't know why, but I had a sudden desire to return to a hotel in Florida where my wife and I had spent our happiest time in our life. I know this was how she felt because she had told me in a letter she left for me after her death.

Though Chicago and Florida were a good distance away I resolved to jump in my car and just drive, sleeping in the car, to visit this hotel (a sort of private pilgrimage). At this point I must say that with the letter my wife had enclosed a framed photograph that she wanted me to remember her by (it was a particularly wonderful photo that captured her beauty before the illness). In this photo she was wearing a dress that she only ever wore on that holiday and was one I liked a lot, it had a white, black, beige and brown pattern, somewhat similar to that you might see on a butterfly.

I arrived at the resort, but could not remember the name of the hotel and it had changed somewhat over the years, so I walked along the beach looking for it. Eventually I spotted the gardens, and the bar where we had spent time watching our children play in the adjacent pool. I crossed the bridge over the rushes and entered the garden. It was then the most amazing thing happened. Hovering in front of me was a butterfly. It just hovered below eye level and continued to do so as I stood there. The butterfly continued to hover and then suddenly soared a foot and its underside was displayed, exposing exactly the same pattern that had been on the dress.

Needless to say, I stood in that garden and sobbed, convinced that my wife was reassuring me that she had indeed found God and was 'soaring like a butterfly on this higher plane'.

As a footnote on my return from the USA I was looking closely at the photo she had left me (as I often do) and I realised something that I had never noticed before, that she was wearing a pendant in the shape of a butterfly around her neck.

Now, I am a rational person. The reason I am attracted to the Baha'i faith is that it is free from superstition. I do believe however that, in some way that I cannot and will not understand until I die, my wife was able to create this sequence of events to give me reassurance after her death.

May, Ontario, Canada

Back in the 1970s, I lived with my parents because of an accident in which my husband was left a quadriplegic. The home I lived in before that was not equipped for a wheelchair. I had moved to my mother's temporarily until I found a place. At the time I owned a part husky, part fox dog called Patches. When I found a place to live, I could not take the dog with me so I left her with my mother. The dog was very close to my mother. One day she was across the road helping a neighbour's dog collect the cows. A car was coming down the road and she heard it coming. Because she was afraid of cars, she ran home. As she crossed the road, she was stuck by the car, and was killed instantly. Now, because of some financial hardships, I had moved back up to my mother's house a few years later. About a year after that my husband wasn't with me anymore and then a few months later my mother was diagnosed with cancer. I remained in the home to care for her. In all the years I was there, I had never seen another dog like Patches in the area.

One year after my mother was diagnosed with her cancer, I had gone into town with my son to get some groceries. It was a rainy day out. The old car I was driving at the time did not take kindly to damp weather. I had got about a mile down the road when the car stalled. It would not start again. I looked out the window of the car towards the house and low and behold, there was a dog that looked exactly like Patches. She was wagging her tail and barking at me and looking towards the house. So I got out with my son, and an umbrella, and started walking towards the house. The dog ran ahead of me, stopping every once in a while to look back to make sure I was following. When I arrived home, I went in to see my mother and she had stopped breathing. I immediately called for an ambulance. When I heard the fire-truck and ambulance sirens coming down the road, I looked outside. There was Patches sitting quite calmly on the front lawn. As the fire-truck turned the corner, she ran off. My mother turned out to be OK, but the dog I believed to be Patches was never to be seen again. She had come back to save her.

Deborah, Queensland, Australia

My mother died of cancer in June 1994. She lived in Hong Kong and I in Sydney. I grew up with her in New Guinea. On 25 May 1994 I had a dream that I can only describe as an omen. A native New Guinean Shaman witch doctor knocked on the door of my Sydney flat. He had a scarf around his neck and just stared at me. I was immediately frightened and shouted at him that he had come to the wrong place. I closed the door and woke up shaking. I knew then that my mother was going to die.

On 30 May my stepfather called from Hong Kong. He told my brother and I to catch a plane because it was time. We arrived the next day. My mother was obviously ready to go, she refused to go to hospital and would not eat or drink except for a little tea. It was a very emotional and sad time for us all. She told me she had had a dream where three girls in flowing tunics and sandals had greeted her to take her across a river – she had said to them that she was no longer thin and ill but normal and well. She said that she saw a city across the river which was the most beautiful place she had ever seen. I told her that this was a great sign and that she should go.

On the night of 2 June we went to bed. She kissed me and said 'I will be there in the morning'.

At 4.48 a.m. on 3 June I was awoken by her voice calling me with great urgency. She called my name three times 'Debbie, Debbie, Debbie.' I jumped up and the door, which was closed, was covered with shimmering gold light. I knew she had gone so I ran to the window. It was sunrise. I then composed myself, had a shower and lay back in bed. I felt very calm and happy that she was released from her suffering. At 6 a.m. my stepfather burst into my room saying that she was gone, but of course I already knew.

Many things happened in the following months – she loved birds and two peach-face finches flew into the apartment circling my stepfather, sitting on his shoulder. They were there for a week and gave him much joy. He found out that they had escaped from an apartment quite far away and he returned them to a very grateful owner. We believe she sent them as a sign from the spirit.

Some months later I was alone at home in Sydney sitting on the bed with a glass of wine. I was feeling very sad, very empty. The room filled with a rose-type scent. An incredible sensation of love, that I cannot adequately describe, emanated from a fixed spot some yards from me. It was as if someone was standing there sending me infinite enveloping love. I couldn't see anything or hear anything, I just sensed this wonderful love. I know it was my mother.

8

A Mother's Love is a Blessing

A mother's love is one of the most important gifts anyone, young or old, can experience. When a mother dies it is often deeply traumatic and roots are so deep the pain of loss is experienced like a toothache in the soul.

The following stories testify to the seamless love of mothers who, having passed over, have returned at significant moments to reassure their children that they are still being cared for and watched over.

Paul, County Kerry, Ireland

My wife, Conchita, was Spanish. She was delighted with her pregnancy, as had never seen herself married and about to start her own family. We met each other in Ecuador in 1986 while working as humanitarian and development volunteers. We were married on Easter Monday 1989 and now, in February 1990, Conchita, aged thirty-three, was about to give birth. She imagined that we might have a family of three or four children.

I could see she loved children and was very excited at the reality of becoming a mother. All those years of being

119

single and not knowing where her future lay were now anxieties of the past. She was very happy in our home, a flat on the North Circular Road, Dublin, Ireland. Learning English was a struggle for her. However she still communicated very well with people and had made many friends during her two years in Ireland.

She was good with her hands and crocheted a blanket for our forthcoming child. I watched as she patiently worked the material until she was happy with the finished garment, working from a design in her head. To finish it she added a border of frills a few inches long. The blanket was put in a bag of items in preparation for childbirth. Conchita was very attentive to her health and that of her unborn child, taking care with her diet, keeping all her doctor's visits, pre-natal appointments, etc. This child was well loved, long before it came into the world. All would be ready.

Her waters broke early in the morning of 15 February, 1990, as predicted. The delivery was relatively short, especially for a first child. Our baby was born a few minutes before one o'clock in the afternoon, a healthy, content child. Conchita held him and wondered what we would call him, as we hadn't decided on a name for a boy. We eventually called him Juan Manuel. He was wide awake, cried very little and seemed to follow the activity around him. Then tragedy struck on that bright, cold spring day. Complication's set in and Conchita was dead by five o'clock. The world fell in on me.

Juan stayed in hospital for the next few days until the funeral arrangements were over and the Spanish relations had gone home. All the while he was wrapped in the blanket his mother had lovingly made for him. This blanket would take on great significance over the years to come as it went everywhere with him – during the day when out and about in his pram and at night when he went to bed. The day he was born I returned to my parent's home in Dublin. They literally saved me. They carried me through my grief as I attempted to come to terms with such a brutal loss. The blanket meant a lot to me too, a connection between Conchita, me and our son, Juan, and a symbol of her love.

In the months that followed, my mother became Juan's mother, a role that was second nature to her. He grew into a happy, lively toddler, full of curiosity and play. One day while I was working, my mother went shopping to the nearby district of Inchicore, as she normally would, and upon her return realised the blanket was missing from Juan's buggy. Horrified at the thoughts of losing such a precious connection she re-traced her steps that afternoon, calling into the shops she had visited and stopping people along the way she knew, in case they might have seen it.

When I came home from work that evening my mother was very upset as she told me that the blanket had been lost. My heart sank, for it was, in truth, one of the most precious links that survived between Conchita and her little boy. I took my bicycle and re-traced the route my mother said she took, but all to no avail. Fortunately, Juan got over the absence of his blanket and we resigned ourselves to the fact that it was gone.

Before we married, Conchita and I were living in my parent's house along with my youngest brother and sister. Having just returned from Ecuador, where I had worked for three years, I still hadn't found a job. There were six adults in the house then, none with a job, until I managed to get part-time work a year later. We registered with Dublin Corporation hoping to get a house or a flat, just long enough to enable us to put down a deposit on a place of our own. Now, having lost Conchita, I approached the corporation again requesting that they reconsider my case in the light of my new situation.

I was listened to sympathetically and a while later, I was advised one Friday that a flat in the neighbourhood would be available the following Monday if I wanted it. It was ideal since it wasn't too far from my parents' house, convenient for minding Juan while I went to work.

There was a lot of cleaning to be done to the flat, as it had been squatted in for the past few years. My father, together with one of my brothers and sisters, volunteered to help me. They rolled up their sleeves and got stuck into cleaning and scrubbing, and throwing out rubbish for the caretaker to remove. At one stage I left to get cleaning materials such as a bucket, mops and disinfectant, etc. and left the others to continue with the work.

Upon my return I noticed they had left a pile of rubbish outside the door of the flat as the caretaker had requested. I was about to pass it when, what appeared to be a filthy rag, caught my attention. I cannot explain what made me stop but something did. My heart raced as I bent down to pick it up. I couldn't believe what I was looking at. There, near the top of the pile of rubbish, was Conchita's lost blanket. I recognised it immediately, even though it was blackened and soiled, but the others hadn't. My sister Jacinta had found it in a coal cupboard and thrown it onto the rubbish heap, just before I returned.

You can imagine my mother's reaction when I arrived home that evening with the blanket. She recognised it immediately without me having to say anything. She lovingly held it, her eyes filled with amazement and disbelief, before putting it in the wash. The next day we gave it back to Juan. He was now two, and the blanket had been gone for over a year. He held it up to his face and fingered the frills as though it was never lost. Juan is now fifteen and to this day the blanket has been in his room and naturally holds a very special significance for him, as it does for me. At the time I was still very confused and hurting. I needed to find it, as much for myself, as for Juan. Some friends said to me at the time, 'Conchita is looking after you', and I believe that. I sensed her loving presence very intimately.

What is the meaning to this story? Is it just coincidence that we found Juan's blanket or is there a deeper dimension to it? For me it seems to suggest that I was meant to live in that flat for a while, that there is a continuum in the sequence of events in our lives if we are attentive to them. Conchita crocheted the blanket, Juan was born, she died and the blanket was lost. Juan and I lived with my parents, we then lived in the flat for two short years, and we then moved on with our lives. Later I met Kathleen, we married, and together we bought a house in Clondalkin, Dublin and life began again.

It is as though for a while in my life I too was briefly lost and then found myself again.

Linda, Ontario, Canada

When I was growing up, unlike other little girls I knew, I had no interest in getting married and having a ceremony. I was not concerned about a frilly white dress and pink flowers and the accoutrements that go along with a wedding. The only two things that were certain in my mind were that I would not get married until I was older and that my mother, an expert and creative seamstress, would make my dress.

When I was twenty years of age my mother died suddenly. Luckily for me, there were no words left unsaid between us and despite the fact that my parents divorced when I was thirteen and I had chosen to live with my father, mom and I knew we loved each other very much. In the seventeen years since her death I have come to understand that she was much stronger than I ever gave her credit for and to recognise her influence over who I am today.

When I became engaged to be married less than a year ago one of the most distressing thoughts in an otherwise happy time was that my mother would not be making my dress and would not be present at my wedding. I was fearful that I would become over emotional thinking about her and would focus on the thought that she was not there to be part of my special day. I could have saved myself a lot of tears because I have no doubt that mom was present at my wedding.

About a week before the 17 April 2004 date I had a final meeting with the manager where we would have our wedding party. For the first time I noticed that on the wall right behind where my husband and I would be sitting was a large picture of a pink tulip, my wedding flower. I mentioned to the manager that it was quite a coincidence because I was going to place a vase full of pink tulips at each guest table. She surprised me by saying that she had only found that picture a few days earlier, dusty and forgotten in the basement and for no particular reason, decided to place it above the fireplace where it now hung.

When I told my fiancée this story he immediately decided it was my mother's intervention that brought that picture out of hiding. From that moment on I felt my mother's presence and strength guiding me.

Only my fiancée knew how frightened I was of walking down the aisle and saying my vows in front of our closest family and friends. I had spent many hours crying, telling him I did not think I could do it. Several times I almost called the whole thing off, terrified that I would have a panic attack or faint in the taking of my vows. I was so frightened during my entire engagement that my fears took away most of the pleasure that planning a wedding is supposed to bring. On the eve of my wedding I felt like a ghost. I made it through the rehearsal but was unable to eat at the family gathering afterwards. That night I could barely sleep. I kept wishing my mother was there to help me. I started to talk to her. I asked her to help me get through the walk down the aisle, the vows and the display without falling apart and I felt her respond, telling me that yes, she would help me. Then I fell asleep. When I awoke, a great sense of calm had overtaken me. I knew my mother was there, guiding me and I felt her spirit with me all day until the final guests left the brunch. Even though she was not physically present the spiritual presence of my mom gave me the strength and courage to start what I anticipate to be a long and happy marriage.

Maeve, County Sligo, Ireland

My dear mum died three years ago. Shortly before she died she was in and out of a coma and my brother and sister-in-law called to see her in hospital. We were all around her bedside, and I whispered in her ear that they had arrived. My brother and sister-in-law had no children and she had two miscarriages. She was now eight weeks pregnant again. I whispered in my mum's ear that they had arrived and with her eyes closed she whispered 'did they bring the baby girl?' and we asked her to say it again, and again she said 'did they bring the little girl?' She died the following week on the 22 June, and the following 22 January, my mum's birthday, my sister-in-law gave birth to a beautiful baby girl!

She was a very generous and kind person, and lived for her family. She would have prayed so much for my sister-in-law and offered several rosaries a day for us all.

Jim and Deborah, San Diego, USA

Jim: I am the youngest of a large family from Belfast and can remember how mum, God rest her, would donate pennies to the Sisters of the Little Flower.

I was very fortunate to visit the reliquary of St Thérèse (The Little Flower), containing her remains, during their visit to Golden Cathedral, when it passed through San Diego. The chapel at the Catholic University was full to capacity and my girlfriend Deborah and I had to stand in the aisles.

Although Deborah had never met my mum, she had seen the one photograph of her which I have carried with me since I left home twenty years ago. As Deborah and I waited and the congregation rotated to receive Holy Communion I saw mum ahead of us waiting in line. She turned and looked straight at me and smiled.

Needless to say I was astounded and, heart racing, I tried to get up behind her. I was torn between elation and anguish as I lost her as quickly as she had appeared.

When Mass was over, Deborah and I left. On the drive home, Deborah, without looking at me, just asked, 'Did you see your mum? I noticed she was wearing that dress you got her.' Deborah actually mentioned it to me first.

The feelings evoked at the time of the incident were real. I've pondered this many times and know that, of all the saints, considering Mum's devotion, Thérèse would have been the most likely catalyst to let me know Mum was in good hands.

Deborah: We were at the viewing of St Thérèse's remains on the morning of Christmas Eve 1999. There was standing room only so we were in an apse. I tend to be an observer when I'm in a crowd and so I was looking around at all the different people when I noticed a diminutive, elderly lady who looked just like the photo of Jim's mom, the only photo of her I've seen. The same floral print dress, the same way her jaw was set. I watched her take Communion and then waited for her to come out the other end of the Communion line because I wanted to get over to her and get a closer look at her.

Even though I watched her intently I didn't see her come out the other end of the line. I immediately started watching both exits, but never caught sight of her again. I looked for her all during the rest of the service and again outside. I had my eyes peeled for her, but she was gone.

Note: This story was first published in Don Mullan's *A Gift of Roses: Memories of the Visit to Ireland of St Thérèse*. In May 2005 we wrote to Jim seeking permission to re-publish the above story. His girlfriend Deborah replied, saying that Jim had passed away two years earlier on 6 May and gave us the necessary permission. 'I'm sure he would love for you to use his story and in a way, this being so close to the anniversary of his passing, I feel like it's one of his little ways of saying "hello" to me, as well.'

In a follow-up email, Deborah wrote: 'Thank you so much for your kind e-mail. I must tell you that it brought comfort and tears to my eyes. Here is another coincidence. Jim's memorial service was held here in San Diego on 18 May 2003, the same date of your last e-mail. I know he is with me always. He has shown himself in so many ways to me and his brother and others that he loved.

'His way seems to be in the finding of pennies in odd places. One in particular I remember vividly. A month or so after he passed on, I had been at my computer and got up and was standing in the living-room and I heard a definite "clink", the sound of metal hitting glass. I was alone in the apartment and it was quiet but the clink was very noticeable. My computer desk has a glass top, so I went back to my desk and there was a penny that had not been there before. I wrote to his brother to tell him about this occurrence and he told me that he had been in the shower and out of nowhere a coin dropped onto the bottom of his tub.

'Jim has sent me and his brother and other members of my family "pennies from Heaven" on numerous occasions since his passing. I love him dearly and I always will. There is not a day goes by that I do not think of him.'

9

In Dreams

What are dreams? Everyone dreams but in most instances we do not remember them. When we do we are often entertained, puzzled and curious as to their deeper meaning. Undoubtedly dreams come from deep within the subconscious mind.

There are many stories from Jewish and Christian scriptures which involve dreams. For example we are told that Joseph, the husband of Mary, had a dream while he was contemplating ending their engagement when he discovered she was pregnant with Jesus. The dream involved an angel who told him not to be afraid to take his expectant fiancée as his wife.

Can dreams, therefore, be the conveyors of messages from beyond? The following writers certainly believe they can.

Brid, County Cavan, Ireland

My husband Pádraig died in a farm accident on a wet October afternoon in 1986. I was at work at the time and so the tragedy wasn't discovered until that evening. At 7 p.m. I went outdoors to see why he hadn't come home. As I called out his name in the darkness, I had a horrible sinking feeling. I knew the worst had happened before I found him. Two days later he was buried – on my eldest daughter's fifth birthday. I was heartbroken. Time passed in a blur of tears. I had lost the person I loved with all my heart and soul, the person I had hoped to grow old with. My children would grow up without knowing the attentive and affectionate man that was their father. The weeks and months following his death were dismal indeed but a number of things happened that gave me some comfort.

I was finding it difficult to sleep at night because every time I closed my eyes I saw him again, lying broken and blood-stained, in the wet farmyard. One night however, utterly exhausted, I fell into a deep sleep. At some point I began to dream. I dreamt that I was sitting alone in our living-room. The door opened and Pádraig walked in. I was shocked when I saw him.

'But you're dead!' I exclaimed.

'Yes', he replied, 'but I want you to know that I'm all right'.

We talked for a while. I was anxious to know if he had suffered – those terrible wounds were plainly visible on his person. He told me that he hadn't. When I awoke the next morning, I felt as if a weight had been lifted from me. There was peace within me where earlier there had been turmoil.

The second incident occurred a few weeks later. His parents called one evening. His mother and I were discussing what we would do with his clothes and other belongings. We decided that certain members of the family might like to keep some mementoes. A few tearful hours later, I was standing at the door saying goodbye to his parents. I became aware of a hand

131

resting on my left shoulder. It had been Pádraig's habit to rest his hand on my shoulder, as we would wave visitors goodbye from our door. I felt his presence strongly as I watched the tail lights of the car disappear down our laneway. I wasn't frightened. I knew that this was his way of telling me that he was still with me.

Johanna, County Wicklow, Ireland

My father died in 1975. Needless to say, we were devastated as it was a sudden passing from this world. All seemed black and gloomy without him. He was an incredible gentle giant of a man and taught us all so much.

One month after his dad's death I went to bed at my usual time. I fell quickly into an exhausted sleep. I started to dream in a very different way. Everything was in twilight. I was going to visit my father's grave in the dream. Upon entering the graveyard I decided to walk the long way around to his grave visiting many of the other people I had known on the way. Edging even closer to my father's grave I began to feel that everything was quite different than before. I felt frightened as I drew closer. Then, as I looked at the headstone I realised that the grave had been dug out. There was no coffin, no remains, nothing. I felt full of grief and wondered what had happened, who could have done this? I felt so troubled and alone and this light was scary, neither light nor darkness just a drab grey.

As I started to despair I heard a very faint calling coming from behind me. I knew it was my father's. He gently called my name until I turned around. There was a tree close by the grave and my father was standing beside it. He looked so welcoming with his arms held out to embrace me. I hurried to be with him. He wore his working clothes, which he always felt most comfortable in; wool polo-neck jumper, navy serge trousers and his work boots. He said he was sorry for startling me but that it was time for him to leave this world, that he was going to a better place and that we would be united again. He told me he was very happy and loved me so much and his last words were 'don't worry'. He gave me a great big bear hug and I never felt such happiness before as I buried my head in his chest. After ages I reluctantly let him go and he walked away from me going in a northern direction and I watched him until he vanished.

When I awoke I felt so completely different than I had before. I was full of his love. His spirit had connected with me at a deeper level. Most importantly I was no longer afraid of death. The fear was gone. I had always been a worrier and da had called me 'his little worrier' but from that day I tried to change and now I don't worry about things. If I can change something for the better I do, if not, I pray and leave it in God's hands.

This experience changed my life. A spiritual bond was formed and I feel my father's presence most of the time but particularly when my life is difficult.

Audrey, County Down, Northern Ireland

As a child, I slept in the same room as my grandmother for the last two years of her life. I used to wake up with a start every time she stopped breathing in her sleep, waiting until I heart her gasping intake of breath, which proved that she still lived. Nobody had told me that it was normal for some old people to do that, so I stayed awake, constantly on the alert, feeling it was my responsibility to protect her.

For as long as I can remember she was bent over with a huge hump on her back. She was so thin that the skin hung between her shoulder blades. She had difficulty walking and was practically blind with cataracts in both eyes. Her move-ments were painfully slow as she forced her arthritic bones into action when every single day, come rain or shine, she went out walking. She said if she didn't do that she would seize up with arthritis and become a bedridden invalid. The thought terrified her and, pain or no pain, there was no way she was going to let that happen.

I was sixteen when she died. The following night, in what I presumed at that time was a dream, I saw her walking to-wards me, her back straight and her eyes clear, and I was strangely afraid at first. I remember stupidly thinking that if she touched me, I would be dead too. This was crazy, because she would never have harmed me. She understood my fear and promised never to scare me like that again. Looking back, I believe it was her way of saying goodbye and to tell me I could relax now, that she was all right and no longer my re-sponsibility. She never entered my 'dreams' again until many years later when I was experiencing a very difficult time, feeling completely alone and not knowing how to go on. Gran and my deceased mother-in-law, who had been my best friend and protector in life, were both in that dream, supporting me on either side. When I awoke I knew I had been given the courage to overcome the problems that had seemed insurmountable the night before. Had they been a figment of my imagination? Was I, by sheer emotion, trying to fulfil my own need? Or had they really come back to support me, by proving I wasn't alone? I still haven't worked that one out, but reasons didn't seem to matter at the time. The two women I have admired the most in my life, came to help me when I was in danger of falling and losing the will to go on.

I am still sceptical though as to whether the dead really do contact us. I suspect it may be our inner selves fulfilling our own needs at traumatic times. But do the reasons really matter, if it gives us the help we need at such times?

Derek, Hampshire, England

I was born on 18 August 1934. I was part of a large tribe and the head of the clan was Jane Towns, known to one and all as 'Big Mother'. Her family was Kate, Phil, George, Walter, May, Ginny and Ada, the latter being my mother.

One by one they passed on, leaving only Auntie May, who was like a second mother to me. I married and moved south, occasionally going home every few years to see all my cousins.

One night I had a dream, in full colour and very vivid. I was walking along a platform at Newcastle Central Station. I came across my 'Big Mother', Kate, Phil, Ginny and my own mother, standing on the platform with all their luggage, suitcases and bags.

I asked in surprise where they were all going – on holiday perhaps?

'No', my mother said, they were waiting for May to arrive. When I woke and realised that they were all on the other side I concluded that my aunt had died. I rang her son Colin immediately but he said no she was alive and well, in fact she was going to the bingo hall that afternoon. I told him of my dream where May's family were waiting for her. He dismissed this as just a dream but a week later he rang to tell me she had died suddenly of a heart attack. So now they were all together again!

Madeline, Dublin, Ireland

Whilst living in Australia in the late 1960s, I had a dream that I was on an airplane and was walking in the aisle between the seats. I saw my sister and my aunt on my left hand side and they greeted me. I answered them. I said, 'I am not really here, just in spirit.' I walked on until I came to a lighted door on my right. Just as I got to it my father stepped through it. We did not speak, but I handed him a cup of coffee that I had in my hand.

His appearance both shocked and upset me. His face was white as chalk and his eyes were red rimmed. He was dressed in a white shirt, open at the neck with his sleeves rolled up. I knew that he was stressed.

The dream upset me very much. I told my husband about it but he just shrugged it off. Five days later I received a letter from my sister telling me that my father had died the week before. They could not tell me sooner because I had no phone at the time.

Three years later I came home to Ireland. I told my sister that I knew the exact date of my father's death, and not only that but I was able to describe his appearance and dress at the time of his death. She was totally shocked and told me that I had described him exactly as he was when he died. He had taken off his jacket and tie and rolled up his sleeves when he began to feel ill. I know that I had a visit from my father when he died or when he was dying.

Pauline, Bolton, England

During the autumn of 1984 I was working on board a cruise ship sailing out of America. At that time I was sharing a cabin with my best friend. One particular night I woke up in a hot sweat after experiencing what I thought to be a nightmare. In the dream my grandmother, who had passed away in 1974 was leaning over my mother in her bed and saying to me that I must come home as my mother was dying. Upon waking I was totally confused as I could not understand why my deceased grandmother was talking to me in a dream about my mother.

Six weeks later my father rang the ship to say I was to come home as my mother was only given a few days to live. I arrived home and my mother was in hospital and went into a coma, from which I thought she would not recover. The next day I visited and she was awake. She kept looking over her shoulder and appeared to be talking to someone I could not see, telling them to go away. She recovered for a while longer and was allowed to go home. Some months later she took another bad turn and was admitted to hospital. Although I knew she was in the best place something told me to go back late that evening out of visiting hours. I sat outside and could hear her crying to come home. I tackled the hospital staff and insisted that she should come home as that was what she wanted. Upon arrival home, as I was getting her ready for bed, she just said 'I have just seen my mum and dad.' She passed away the very next day.

I was also there when my father passed away and just before he drew his last breath on earth I saw the most beautiful light in his eyes, which I believe was the light of God taking him home.

Denise, Kent, England

A couple of years ago I had a repetitive dream of seeing my family, on my dad's side, together at a funeral. I could see my dad clearly as a mourner but couldn't see who was missing. A few months later my uncle Tom, dad's brother, died very quickly after a stroke. Going back to my dream, I remember seeing dad sitting in a waiting-room at a crematorium not wanting to leave.

I was later told by my brother that when they turned off uncle Tom's life support Dad had refused to leave him. This must have been what I was seeing in my dream when dad didn't want to leave the waiting-room.

Twenty-five years ago when I was seventeen, my nan went into hospital. I believed it was just for something routine, so I wasn't too concerned. The truth was she was very ill but my parents kept this from my brother and me.

This particular night my mother was visiting nan and arranged to stay for a few days. At 11.30 p.m. I awoke, having just had a heartbreaking dream in which my nan had come to me to say goodbye because she had passed over.

Dad told me to stop being silly and to go back to sleep. At 6 a.m. the following morning mum called dad to say that nan had passed over about 11.30 p.m. the previous night!

Chris, Stockport, England

I believe that the dead have communicated with me. Two of my close friends died, the first in 1991 and the second in 1998. Whilst I feel that both communicated with me it is the latter that may be of more interest to you.

In March 1998 my best friend Garry crashed his motorcycle. He lived for just a few hours, long enough for me to get to the hospital. I was with him when they turned off the life support machine and he died.

I had the normal grief and dreamt about him as is usual I suspect. However, one morning I had an extremely vivid dream. I remember this particularly well because my girlfriend of the time and I were going to V98, a rock festival, on that day. The dream was so strong that I wrote it down and dated it.

In the dream I was walking through my house when the phone rang. I picked it up and it was my friend Garry. In the dream it seemed perfectly normal that Garry could and would call me and we spent a minute or two telling corny jokes to each other. Then he said 'I have something I want to give you'.

I asked him what it was but he wouldn't tell me. He said he wanted it to be a surprise. He said that the item he wanted to give me was in the pocket of his long black coat. At this point it encroached on my awareness that he was dead but it still seemed acceptable that he could communicate in this way. I told him that I missed him and that I wanted to thank him for getting in touch with me and thank whoever else made it possible for him to do so.

He said that he had to go. I asked him what it was like to be dead but the line was silent.

I woke up and immediately wrote the dream down. I went to V98 with my girlfriend and didn't think much more about it until a few days later. I phoned Garry's fiancée. In the intervening months we had grown more friendly as I had spent some time comforting her through this difficult time. I tentatively told her about my dream. She said that she thought she had searched through all Garry's clothes but would do so again. She recognised the long black coat as an actual coat of Garry's. She phoned back about ten minutes later to say that she had found a pendant in the pockets with what looked like hands in a praying position. She sent the pendant to me. The hand position she mentioned is actually a Kung-Fu greeting and is a left vertical hand against a right fist. I still have the pendant. I have had many dreams about Garry that I sense are more than just imagination but there is no way I could prove it.

Michelle, County Cavan, Ireland

Several years ago something strange happened to me and has stayed with me. At the time we were living in America and we were home visiting my husband's family in Cavan. One night I had a very bad dream in which I heard crying. I woke up shaking and explained the dream to my husband. The next day I took my daughters and nieces to Dublin for the day. On the bus home the girls asked me why I was so very close to my grandfather. I explained to them that I had lived with my grandparents and they cared for me very well as a child. When my husband came to collect us in the town he said he had very bad news and that my grandfather had died in Philadelphia several hours ago.

10

Sense and Sensibility

In this chapter testimonies state that while deceased loved ones and friends did not actually appear, they did, however, manifest themselves through whispered words or sounds that made the hearers aware of their presence. Remarkably, sometimes these sounds were heard across oceans, on the far side of the earth, and hearers claim they knew that a deceased one had come to say goodbye.

If true, it suggests that the dead are not dead and in dying have been released from the limitations of time and space.

Emma, County Limerick, Ireland

My father-in-law died in September 2002. He was a warm and charismatic man, a publican, historian, army captain, and the father of four sons.

He had been ill after a stroke and, as often happens, waited for the fourth son who was in New York to return before he 'let go'. He died alone with this son after the family had spent all day with him on and off in varying combinations. We returned to the hospital where he was laid out and prayers were said. We drove the thirty miles home. In the middle of the

142

night I woke with a brilliant light flooding the room. At first I though burglars must have turned the lights on, but my husband slept on. I felt a sudden ease and understanding after my initial shock at the light. It was intense, vibrated in the room and a sense of peace pervaded. I 'knew' what or who it was and I just turned over and slept. When I woke it was the first thing I recalled.

My sister-in-law from New York who came with her husband related that exactly twelve hours after John had died there was a soft tap-tap-tap on all the windows in the house – including upstairs – just the way John knocked at the house when visiting them on holiday. They looked up and down the street at the time but of course the streets were empty.

Moira, Perthshire, Scotland

My husband dropped dead on holiday in 1977, at the age of forty-two. I was just thirty-eight at the time. Of course there were no goodbyes and I was left destroyed by grief. I put on a wonderful act at the office during the day, showing I was coping well but returned to a big empty house in the evening and just exploded into floods of tears, until I was making myself physically sick. This went on for months.

On one of those occasions I was sitting at the dressing-table in our bedroom, on which lay a small cassette player which had belonged to my husband. It had never been used since his death. In the midst of my uncontrollable sobs, some force made me, unwillingly, reach out an arm and press the 'play' button. The machine contained a hysterical tape by the Scots comedian Billy Connolly, which my husband had bought shortly before he died. Within seconds I was helpless with laughter. I could almost hear my husband say 'Don't you think you have cried enough – have a laugh for a change!' My road to recovery started right there.

Albert, New South Wales, Australia

On a visit to Perth, Western Australia – my former home town – after many years absence, I wondered if I would encounter a man that I had worked with in a furniture factory many years before.

I had no idea if he was alive or dead. I dreaded the thought of meeting up with him again.

He was a decent enough fellow but an absolute pest. He always had to know everything about me, what my parents did, how much money they had, how much money I had. He didn't approve of the make of the watch that I wore and one day ripped it off my wrist and tossed it into the garbage bin. This is just a small example.

During our trip to Perth, my wife and I decided to go to the cemetery to visit my parents' graves. It is a huge cemetery and as I had not been there for many years it was quite daunting.

Whilst we were looking I accidentally slammed my foot on the corner of a grave. The pain was excruciating. I bent down to rub my foot and as I stood up I looked at the tombstone. Yes, there it was, his grave.

Now if you knew this chap as well as I had known him, you would swear that this was his way of saying, 'Hey Albert, this is where I am.'

I am not a believer generally but I am convinced he tried to make contact. He was just being his usual painful self.

Bairbre, County Donegal, Ireland

The subject of the connection between those who have died and ourselves is of great interest to me. I have had some experience in this area. My mother died when I was five and my brother died at the age of twenty-two when I was eighteen. I have a very strong sense of them around me and am particularly aware of my mother's input in my life. My young niece has also had the experience of my mother coming to comfort and reassure her after the trauma of emigration to America.

My own most vivid experience occurred some fourteen years ago. Before we married my husband studied in Chicago. While there he worked with the Native American community and came to know a young girl suffering from cancer. For many months he gave blood platelets for her. At the age of five this little girl died. Some months later I was at a Mass in the college where I was studying. At the Eucharistic prayer we were all standing up around the altar. I became aware that Aguasuk, the little Native American girl, was in the space behind me, laughing and dancing. I did not 'see' her and yet I simply knew she was there. When I later told my future husband about my experience he said a number of

145

people had experienced Aguasuk and each one had reported her as 'laughing and really dancing'.

She had loved to dance and this was something that became impossible for her, as the cancer had progressed. To me it was a really positive and life-affirming experience and in no way scary or ghostly.

Lorraine, California, USA

I believe my father's spirit is still around. My Dublin-born father passed away on Saturday 15 June 2002, the day before Father's Day, just after 7 p.m. My parents emigrated to southern California in 1959 after two years in Toronto. Though my dad loved the opportunity and sunshine of California, he was very connected with the goings on back in his hometown of Dublin where his many brothers and sisters live.

Several weeks before dad passed on, he would wake up in the middle of the night singing old Irish tunes in a full strong voice. By day, dad could barely whisper, due to his declining health. The night before dad died he didn't sing and my older brother Dermot felt that he was near to death. Dad died at home in his bed with my younger brother Paul and my mother present.

Last Christmas Day my family was at the table having Christmas dinner. A bit of a row was starting and we were all becoming defensive. Then a door slammed and it quieted us all down. We felt that it was dad's way of walking away from the fuss, which he used to do when he was alive.

11

Someone to Watch over Me

These stories relate to both deceased relatives and special friends and, as the name suggests, they relate to incidents or experiences whereby an individual feels the strong presence of someone or they feel someone is literally watching over them.

Barry, Nova Scotia, Canada

As soon as the condom broke I knew something could well be very wrong. Although I had had a few beers I was very sober while I went home by taxi, crossing the MacDonald Bridge from Dartmouth to Halifax, Nova Scotia, in the wee hours of the morning. The driver, a Russian, told me all about life in St Petersburg and how it compared to life in eastern Canada. I heard his voice, but none of what he was saying made any sense. I was thinking to myself: I might have been just exposed to HIV and I might die of AIDS in ten years, or less. Does my insurance pay for treatment? Was fifteen minutes of sex really worth the fear I would encounter for the next several months of not knowing if I was positive or not?

On Monday morning I went to see my doctor. He immediately sent me for a blood test and later that week I was told it was negative. 'We'll have to check you in about three months just to be sure,' he said. My fear was so overwhelming that it felt like a big snake coiled around my whole body. I started to look at people differently. Why do people gossip and say mean things about one another when life and death is as thin as the line between madness and brilliance? What is it like when a woman is told she has breast cancer, or a man is told he has prostate cancer? All I knew is that if God allowed me not to be HIV positive that I would give up my life to follow His rule and help others somehow – however He wanted me to meet His calling. I prayed everywhere – in silence in my head when I was with other people, through tears when I was alone, and in whispers when I was taking showers.

I even found when I was singing, walking in a park, I would be suddenly praying words. In short, I felt so alone and the few people I told my misfortune to told me not to worry about it and that in fact I was probably all right yet I kept thinking about my doctor's words: 'Just to be sure you need to be tested again.'

Three months of hell went by. Sometimes I would go to sleep with my head so heavy I could hardly breathe. I would read books but the print was just ink on paper; they didn't make any sense. Magazines were just glossy papers and advertisements and commercials on television seemed almost like comics in a fantasy world where only the healthy lived, and lived only temporarily until misfortune took hold of them.

I started to think a lot about my father. He had committed suicide in 1989, at the age of fifty-six. He had been in the army and drank heavily and finally the alcohol seized him. He finally took a gun and ended his life after sending my mother to the store for chocolate milk.

Three months later I was sitting in my doctor's office again waiting for the results of my HIV blood test. A woman was sitting in the waiting-room reading a magazine while her little blond boy was peeking in through the screen door of the deck where smokers could go. The boy pressed his face against the screen door and his eyes stared at mine. Then he stuck his tongue out and slid it along the plastic screen. Then he'd move his head. He was having a cat and mouse game with me and although I was full of fear, I had to chuckle a few times at this play. His mother finally looked up and saw what he was doing and made him stop. I got up and went to the bathroom to put cold water on my hot face.

Beside myself, I started to cry, hard, and I leaned my face down and cupped water onto my face. I didn't know how I was going to have the strength to find the answer to whether I would eventually get AIDS or not.

Then I looked up into the mirror. Then I saw my father's face; he was standing behind me in a blue shirt and he was smiling. 'It's okay,' he said. 'You're going to be okay, Barry.'

I turned to talk to him but he was gone. I looked in the cubicle and even behind the door. No one was there. I walked out into the waiting-room and the woman and her boy were gone. The office door opened and my doctor took me to a room and closed the door. 'Everything is okay, Barry.'

Again, I started to cry, but this time in happiness. 'I know,' I said. 'My father just told me.'

Charles, Cheshire, England

I was in bed one night and finding real sleep difficult, as it was only some three weeks since my wife's funeral. I lay on my back with my arms and hands on my chest. It was completely dark and suddenly I felt a presence sit heavily on the bed. Almost immediately it lay squarely on top of me and I felt both of my hands being forcibly gripped and squeezed. At this point I tried to call out in fear, but only managed to moan. The presence then rolled to my side where my wife would normally have been and I perceived it to be her, although I couldn't see her. She then rapidly went away. It was as if she wanted me to know she was all right. I found sleep even more difficult for the rest of the night.

Other experiences were also inexplicable. My wife and I used to sit in separate armchairs next to each other while watching television in the evening. I disliked commercial breaks and often fell asleep during them. If we were watching some epic picture or serial, once the programme resumed my wife would give me a forcible dig in the ribs to awaken me. Following her death, if I was watching television on my own and fell asleep during the commercials I felt her dig me in the ribs to awaken me. This happened on a number of occasions.

I had another unusual experience when I was working in Manchester. I was always early and there was one particular man who was a cleaner in the department. We always exchanged morning pleasantries; he was a very affable person. His name was Joe and one morning in the winter-time I arrived at my workplace and saw Joe standing between some machinery. I shouted my usual greeting 'Good Morning Joe'. He would always reply with some comment about the weather but on this occasion there was no reply. I repeated my greeting but still received no answer. I then continued into the locker room where I met one of his colleagues. I asked 'What's the matter with Joe this morning? I couldn't get a word out of him.'

Joe's colleague looked at me with a puzzled expression and said 'What are you talking about, he died last night.'

I didn't know what to say, and moved quickly away. I told no one about my experience.

Beth, Cumbria, England

The deceased I talk of is my son's dad Jeff. I am now twenty-seven years old; Jeff was twenty-five years of age when he took his own life four and a half years ago. At the time I was four and a half months pregnant with our son.

Ours was a complicated relationship. He had a partner who was regularly being unfaithful. We had been out in our teens, then met up again this last time, we'd not seen each other in between times. He'd confided in me about her affair. He came to visit me a few times and had cried. I told him I still loved him. We only slept together once, and there was our son.

I tell you all this to try to give some background. We

were together in all for nine months. I told him I was pregnant and he decided he wanted to be with me. After that, he left me saying 'the next time you see me I will be moving in'. He said he loved me and then proposed to me. I never saw him again.

I stayed single until near on the end of my pregnancy when an ex-boyfriend, asked me if he could be with me and my son. We had gone out previously for four years on and off. Our son Michael was born and small things began to happen, doors opening by themselves, windows shutting, television turning over, lights on and off. Then it got to someone stroking my neck, the cats meowing loudly and the sound of my boyfriend's and son's voices. As my son became more aware he and the cats would focus on a certain part of the livingroom. I have a sixth sense, I can't see them but I 'feel' they are there. So far I have not been wrong.

Then I believe Jeff started moving furniture under my boyfriend when he sat down. This scared him a lot. The worst thing Jeff did to him was he tried to push him down the stairs. After that I started going to my local church. Someone even came to my home to tell Jeff he was not allowed to do this. They said he wished he hadn't killed himself and was jealous of my boyfriend. They described him to me and they were 100 per cent accurate.

I believe Jeff comes to play with Michael. I know when Jeff is here and Michael also tells me 'daddy is visiting'. Once my son was in his room laughing and talking whilst I was in the bath. I got out and asked who he was talking with; he

152

was about three years of age at the time. He said I wasn't allowed to know because I may get upset. So I said 'is there a photo you can show me of who it is?' and he took me downstairs to Jeff's picture. He said 'He doesn't like seeing you crying' before I had explained who Jeff was to Michael. He'd had a spell of two months sleeping in my room because when he'd slept on his own, a man always stayed in there with him. It took me two months to get him to acknowledge that daddy wouldn't hurt him. I explained that he comes to visit to see how his little boy is growing so big.

Charlotte, Cumbria, England

My best friend Johanna died after a long illness in August 2002. She left behind a husband, Scott, and three children. We were always together as one big family. We went on holidays together and were each other's bridesmaids, godparents to each other's children, etc. In fact we were like sisters, as we were both only children and had grown up next door to each other. Each Christmas we always spent Boxing nights as one big get-together, children included. As the children got older this was still the case.

On the first Boxing night after she died – 2002 – we were all together as usual in my house. We were talking about the good times we had had and how we all missed her. It was very late when everyone left and I began to tidy up. I noticed how there seemed to be a strange kind of energy in the house, as though she was in the next room.

I went to bed and quickly fell asleep. I was woken just

before dawn by someone touching my arm. I don't know the exact time. I got out of bed and I seemed to be still asleep because I couldn't open my eyes and yet I could see myself in bed. All my senses were alert but I still could not open my eyes.

She came to me and gave me a hug; she looked well and just like she looked at about twenty-seven years of age. I asked her if I was dreaming. She said that I was not. We then had the following conversation:

    Me: Where are you now?
    J: In heaven.
    Me: What is it like?
    J: It's lovely. Look!

She took hold of my hand and it was like she was pulling back a curtain with her other hand and I glimpsed a lovely sunny garden, albeit very briefly. She said that earth bound people could not see heaven but that she had shown me an image.

    Me: Are you happy?
    J: Yes.
    Me: What do people do there?
    J: They have work to do just as on earth. Everyone does what they are good at.
    Me: Do you work?
    J: No, not yet. I am not fully recovered yet but I will when I am well.

Me: What will you do?

J: Sort of the equivalent of office work on earth.

Me: It's so lovely to see you. I am so sad because you're not here.

J: That's why I came but I have to go now. I am going to see my children. I am going tonight while they are asleep but I will come again.

I then went back into my sleeping self and opened my eyes, but the room was dark and there was no one there. I felt so much better. I wondered if it really had been a dream but dreams tend not to make much sense and this was so tangible. I felt her and saw her and she answered all my questions. I have seen her since but very briefly and she came and went very quickly without speaking; she just smiled at me and disappeared.

The day after my first experience I went to a party and found myself talking to a stranger and somehow recounting my experience. I thought she would think I was mad but she said she had once had a similar experience. I still believe to this day that the combined energy generated by all of us that night was strong enough to help her to come to us. We have not been all together since then but I hope that when we are the same thing will happen.

I spoke to her children after that night and they told me that there was a knocking on the front door and when their father answered there was no one there. Then there was a knocking on the back door – still no one there. They believe it was their mother. I asked them what time this had happened and was told it was about 3.30 a.m.

12

Coincidental

*Coincidence? Of course, there is every possibility that many of the
stories related in this chapter concur with a dictionary definition:
'a chance occurrence of events remarkable either for being simul-
taneous or for apparently being connected'. However, for those
who share their stories below there is a deeper dimension than
mere chance. It is, indeed, a moment when time and eternity em-
braced and what appeared to be broken by death, revealed itself as
whole and everlasting.*

Anonymous, Belfast, County Antrim, Northern Ireland
It was the first anniversary of my father's death in Canada.
He died suddenly last year in hospital after coming through a
triple bypass operation. He was sixty-four, in very good shape
and due to get out of hospital when his heart simply stopped
beating in the middle of the night. His doctors were shocked
and the autopsy could find no reason other than heart fail-
ure. Maybe the trauma of the surgery was too much. I prefer
to believe it was simply his time.

I live in Belfast but my mother and three brothers live in
Canada. As it was my father's anniversary I knew my mother

and brothers were going to an anniversary Mass at 8.30 a.m. (1.30 p.m. Belfast time). I decided to go to St Malachi's Mass at 1 p.m. I needed to get to a meeting at 1.30 p.m. so I left the church early and checked my watch. It was exactly 1.30 and I was thinking that my father's Mass would be starting in Toronto.

Later that night I was speaking by phone to my brother in Toronto and we were chatting away. When I hung up I looked at my watch to see what time it was and it still said 1.30. My watch had stopped as I left the church. I called my brother back to tell him and he reminded me dad was also found dead at 1.30. Then he laughed and said, 'Well thanks for freaking me out.'

After my dad died, we had a dream about him and it seemed to help each of us. My dream was that he came back to tell me he was fine and I poured my heart out about how awful the whole thing was, having to go to the funeral, etc. My mother said he turned up in his best blazer in her dream and she was giving out to him about leaving her high and dry when he said, 'No, I'm always with you' and gave her a hug. My other brother had a dream about my dad too. He asked him if he was in Heaven and he said yes. When my brother asked him about death and what had happened he said, 'I can't tell you that'.

Maybe it is just the mind's way of coping but sometimes I do think when someone dies suddenly their spirit is allowed to hang around a bit to make sure you are all right.

Shulie, London, England

My father was dying of cancer. I left his bedside on a Sunday evening in early July in the knowledge that we had said our final goodbye. It was some time after ten, on the following Friday morning that I was standing at the window in a room at the back of the house overlooking the garden, braced against the inevitable news but feeling oddly serene. Even though my dad was at the very front of my thoughts and I was in tears almost hourly, the tears I shed in that moment were involuntary and sudden. I went back to my own room to finish crying in private. Then I walked over to the book-shelf and picked out a book, one that my dad had lent to me. Leafing through it I found a short poem, which I read through three or four times finding comfort in the words which ended with this beautiful image of a prayer asking God to wrap the old star-eaten blanket of the sky around me.

As I returned the book to its shelf I found myself won-dering why, when I had had this book for so many years and looked through it so many times, had I not noticed this poem before?

Later on that day my mother arrived to tell me the news I had been dreading. My father was gone. He had died that morning sometime between ten and eleven o'clock.

When I went back to my dad's home the day before the funeral his partner and I sat quietly together. Without hav-ing made any conscious decision to do so, I found myself tell-ing her about finding the poem. Since I could not remember the title or the author, I started to describe the imagery and

159

tell her of the feeling it gave me. She interrupted me; she knew instantly what I was taking about. The poem that I had found was his current favourite and because my dad liked to commit poetry to memory as he had done when still a schoolboy, she had learnt it too. She recited the whole piece back to me. Neither of us was astonished by the extraordinary coincidence as anyone might imagine. It just felt normal.

The memory of this incident is something I treasure. I was very close to my father and poetry was something we shared.

Ulo, New South Wales, Australia

My dear friend Billy and I were so close that we would know what we were thinking and respond to such thoughts without a word being uttered. This may be known as co-dependency by some, but to us we were just extremely close. I cared for him physically and emotionally for many years through his battle with HIV. During this time I connected to Pay TV and asked him if he would like me to record anything for him. He replied 'anything with Elizabeth Taylor' which I dutifully did for years, never missing anything, by daily combing though the programme guide to seek out Liz.

We often laughed and pondered what happens to all those programmes sent through the airways to our homes and would laugh that we'd probably be able to access all the reruns of I Love Lucy up there in Heaven.

Our closeness in my opinion clearly meant that if anyone could give me the 'sign' that there is something after death, it would be Billy, and given his declining health I asked him if he would take the time, if he did manage to get there, to let me know that the great dance floor in the sky did in fact exist. 'No,' he replied in his usually cheeky manner. This I knew meant yes, but only when he wants to and not because it was commanded of him. Needless to say, Billy died.

The habit of scouring the TV guide daily was something that took some time for me to wean myself off but I succeeded. I also would hold the remote control in my hand at all times while watching television with a tape in the recorder, on the alert to press record for 'anything with Elizabeth Taylor' that came through unannounced. This habit also faded.

One day while watching nothing in particular I had a sudden unexplained urge to pick up the remote control, turn on the television, tune to a channel that I never ever watch and hit the record button.

The screen burst into *I Love Lucy* with special guest star Elizabeth Taylor. I was in heaven for those thirty minutes as Billy and I enjoyed a rerun.

Derek, New South Wales, Australia

A friend of thirty years, Tom, died of cancer over ten years ago. He put up a good battle and lived a comparatively normal life right up to the end. My wife and I returned from a short holiday and had our evening meal a little later than usual. I did the washing up while she was unpacking. I was alone at the sink when I felt two quite sharp tugs from behind on the upper left arm of my shirt. I automatically turned around thinking it was my wife but there was no one there.

Something felt a bit odd, but after a while I dismissed it. However I did note the time of the incident on the kitchen clock as 8.40 p.m.

Early the next morning my friend's wife rang to say that Tom had died the previous evening in the local hospital. I immediately thought about what happened, then asked if by chance she knew the time of death. She said she was at his bedside when he suddenly stopped breathing and she didn't know why but she had noted the time as exactly 8.40 on her watch. Tom saying goodbye to me or a coincidence?

I still don't know if I believe in an afterlife or not and I am not a regular churchgoer. I have not received any kind of communication from my wife who died three years ago or from any other relatives. However my two daughters swear that their mother is still looking out for them.

Juckle, Liverpool, England

Some years ago a lady I knew called Joyce Sergeant died. She was a very psychic woman and could feel the presence of her mother and father around the house. She used to go to the spiritualist church in Liverpool and was contacted by her husband who asked her why she had removed the roses.

She suffered from bad legs and wasn't able to walk far. One day my husband was standing at a bus shelter at the top of our road and he felt compelled to turn around. He saw Joyce standing behind him wearing the same hat and coat that she used to wear. She spoke to him and said ,'I like it here, I can walk'. My husband opened his mouth to speak and she just vanished. When he came home his heart was pounding and he was quite upset about it as she was a very nice lady. When he thought about it he said she appeared to be floating.

Denis, Wolverhampton, England

When I first retired, my wife and I made a habit of going for a pub meal on pension day.

One week we decided to try the fare at a country hotel. While eating the meal I noticed a fellow eating alone at a nearby table and said 'I'm sure I know him, he used to live next door when I was a lad and then he and his parents moved away after a few years. I'm sure his name is Eric'.

Having finished his meal he walked to our table and said, 'aren't you Denis?'

I said 'yes and you must be Eric. It must be fifty years since we last met.'

We exchanged experiences of the previous years and then he said he had to go into hospital at the weekend for tests relating to a lung problem.

As he left we wished him good luck and said we would to the hotel on the following Thursday and look out for him.

The following week, my daughter and I visited a spiritualist church we had been to once before and the procedure was for the medium to hold a possession like a watch or bracelet and make contact with anyone on the 'other side'. As she held my watch she said she felt difficulty breathing and asked me if I knew of someone very recently passed over. I said no and then she said 'does the name Eric mean anything?' At that moment it really didn't register.

Two days later on the Thursday, my wife and I went to the hotel again for lunch. Whilst ordering the meal the waitress said, 'What a shame about Eric'.

I asked why.

She said, 'He died in hospital at the weekend'.

That was quite a shock, not only his death but to make contact within two days via a medium.

Josephine, County Dublin, Ireland

I was a night nurse for many years, mostly nursing elderly people. About twenty-five years ago one of my patients, a tiny little lady whom I knew had had a hard life, was very ill. We knew she didn't have much time left. One of her feet was gangrenous and the odour permeated the ward.

I was with her when she drew her last breath and as I said the prayers for the dying, I noticed that the awful odour was gone and the smell of roses flooded the ward. It stayed until the remains of the little lady was taken to the mortuary.

Later while collecting her belongings, I found on her locker a picture and a prayer to Padre Pio. I have no doubt that he kept the vigil with me that night.

Frances, County Kerry, Ireland

In 1957 my husband and I we moved to Toronto and it was heartbreaking to leave my mother but we had three children so it was necessary to make a living. We were four years there and writing to mother was our only communication but in February of 1961, whilst coming home from church, I had an overwhelming desire to call my mother. I asked my husband if I could. He said yes. I phoned and my brother answered. When I asked how mother was he said, 'I was just about to contact you. If you had phoned a half hour ago I would have said she was fine but she has just died.' Needless to say that was all I said to him as I was overcome with grief.

Gerti, Vienna, Austria

Are love letters also sent from Heaven? My story is about a love letter from my late husband. However, before I begin my story about the letter, I want to tell you how I met my husband, who was a very unique person.

My friend Heidi invited me to a costume ball in Vienna, my hometown – and also sorted out our costumes. I was Pablo Picasso in a baggy pair of pants, flat shoes and with Pullmann-kappe on high hairstyle – not really very gorgeous, in contrast to Heidi. She was in a long blue and orange gown, as my model.

I had planned a skiing trip to Switzerland a couple of weeks later to meet my then boyfriend, so I did not have very high expectations for the fancy dress ball.

On the night of the ball, at around midnight, I ran into a man, who also was dressed up as an artist and he invited me

165

for a coffee. During our conversation I discovered that he was at the event with half his family, including his mother, and that he was a photographer for the Austrian newspaper, *Die Presse*. He said he thought I looked absolutely beautiful in my costume and took pictures of me. He also asked me if I would be interested in going on an assignment with him the next day.

He was supposed to take a picture in the Ethnology Museum and he thought I could be the foreground of the picture. I liked the idea and agreed to meet him the next day in a coffee-house around the corner from where I lived. Back then I still lived with my uncle, the brother of my father, who took care of my sister and I after our parents had to flee because of the Second World War.

The next day I remembered that I was to attend a birthday party for my nephew. I rushed around the corner to cancel my arrangements with the photographer but he was not there, so I decided to go back home. I was disappointed but also kind of relieved because of the family situation.

The photographer, Heinz, was there but in reality I just had not seen him, so he decided to find out what happened to me. He was sure I must have had a good reason not to show up, so he started looking for me. I had told him I lived around the corner and he knew our street had only seven buildings. On top of that he already had pictures of me from the night before so he was hopeful of finding me.

He decided to go to all the buildings and ask the people if they knew me. He was sitting in his car in front of the first

166

building when he saw an older couple coming down the street and decided to start his quest with them. He asked them if they knew a young, brown-haired girl named Gerti who lived around here and who was waiting for his delivery of her photographs. The couple looked at each other and smiled. It was my parents on their way to the birthday party!

So we met again and we also went to take pictures in the museum. Many more pictures followed and sixteen months later we were married.

So, now the story of my love letter. It was written in 1966 but only found seventeen years later.

Heinz was a press photographer. He and I have always been passionate 'snap shooters'. We decided to take our first trip together to the beautiful Austrian city of Salzburg. At a stunning fountain that originally was used to wash horses, he decided to take a picture of us. Back then we were still using black and white. I set up the camera to make a self-exposure of us in front of a big painting of horses behind the fountain that we liked a lot. Heinz offered to process the film for me after our return to Vienna and I gladly accepted.

When he brought me the prints a little time later I asked him to make me an enlargement of my favourite picture of us together at the fountain. When he finally gave me the photo, it was not only bigger but also, to my surprise, beautifully framed.

The picture had a very special place on the wall of my room at my uncle's apartment and later in our bedroom after we were married.

We were married for fifteen years and the picture was never replaced as it was a testimony to the beginning of our love. We went back to the fountain many times on return trips to Salzburg and always took pictures, including with our son and many friends.

In 1981 my beloved husband Heinz died suddenly. I was devastated and it took me two years to slowly get back on my feet. I was in deep depression but as part of my recovery I decided to change the tapestry in our bedroom. One day, as I took our picture from the wall, it slipped out of my hands. Remarkably, the glass didn't break but the frame was damaged. I was upset about my clumsiness and took the frame apart. To my amazement I found a letter on the back of the picture. It was from Heinz. I read:

> My dear, best, dearest Spatz [the German word for sparrow] I do not know when and if you will ever read these words. I wish in any case, that we will be, at least, as happy as we are now and that we understand each other as much as we do today.
>
> I love you,
>
> Your Mutz [his nickname]
> Vienna
> February 1966

I held the letter very close to my heart and cried. It was Heinz's way of healing me. It wasn't just a coincidence. The letter reassured me he was still close to me. His words gave me the courage to continue.

The picture remained unframed and it has sat next to

my bed for the last twenty-two years. My son asked me for it but even though it was hard not to grant him his wish, I could not part with it ...

After such an event does one not have to believe in ever-lasting love, in small miracles, in heavenly, magic powers?

I do.

Epilogue

When I was twelve years of age my classmates and I were given
a school retreat. One of the people who directed it was Larry,
a larger than life attractive character with guitar in hand who
effortlessly aroused our interest in a subject we, typically as
teenagers, were not impressed by. Religion at the time was to
me and many of my friends just another subject in school. It
wasn't one that presented many challenges or made us contemplate the bigger questions in life but somehow through
laughter and through the telling of his own at times difficult
life story, Larry made us realise how our relationship with God
could impact upon our lives. Hearing first hand the suffering
he had endured at the hands of others and how he had
successfully turned that hurt into something positive, made
me yearn for just a fraction of the inner peace and self belief
that he had found.

Larry exuded a warmth and energy that both captivated
us and encouraged us to share our feelings, thereby gaining a
greater awareness of our own spirituality and our relationships with God. I knew I had met someone special, so much
so that I went home and wrote in my diary about Larry and
the way in which he had changed my perspective. At that
time I could not have known how significant those words
would be.

A few years later I needed my faith more than ever when I became ill with a brain tumour. It was a lengthy and traumatic time but I came through it largely in thanks to the belief Larry had helped me rediscover and nurture.

After a while Larry went his way and I went mine but I never forgot him. Some time later I heard his familiar voice on the radio. That special man from long ago had found his way back into my life again through the power of the airwaves. I was amazed and wrote to him immediately, re-igniting a warm and strong friendship. We got to know each other all over again. We didn't see each other that often but remained in regular contact and he nurtured in me my great love of writing. He had faith in my ability long before I did, providing me with an outlet for my poetry via his weekly radio programme.

Then life dealt a cruel blow. Larry became seriously ill. I often called out to visit him at home, usually phoning first to make sure he was there. Once, on the off chance, I visited and though he'd clearly lost weight, he still had that twinkle in his eye and told me he'd got the all clear. He even joked about saying goodbye to me in his usual mischievous way and I never imagined that that would be the last time I'd ever see him.

Just a few weeks later I got the terrible news that not only had Larry passed away but that I'd missed his funeral as well. I was distraught and felt I'd let him down. He had been one of my best friends and I hadn't said goodbye to him.

Over the years I had often recorded some of his radio programmes and decided to listen to one. By chance I picked up a random cassette and pressed 'play'. It was an excerpt of Larry addressing a youth conference in Dublin. Hearing his voice filled me with both sadness and joy. It reassured me immensely to close my eyes and picture myself back there in the crowd, watching him speak animatedly, his face lighting up with each word. Yet the picture was tinged with grief as I realised that I would never see his face again. I continued to listen, transfixed, as Larry recounted a story I had never listened to before. He told of a young girl he had befriended some years ago whilst giving a retreat in her school.

Some years after the retreat he returned to the area and decided to call to surprise her. He found her home in darkness. A neighbour saw him and said that the couple there had moved away 'because of what had happened'.

'What happened?' he asked. He was told that the girl, his friend, had died in a car accident. Larry was distraught and like me that very day, filled with grief and guilt because he hadn't paid his respects by attending her funeral. He hadn't been there for her, just like I hadn't been there for him. His grief echoed mine, his pain echoed mine. For a moment he walked in my shoes. He was me – shattered and lifeless. It sent a shiver down my spine. Here was the person I felt I had let down, voicing my feelings, my heartache – because he'd been through it himself. He went on to say that in time he began to understand that perhaps God hadn't meant for him to be at the funeral, that maybe it would have been too painful for him. I took great comfort from that.

172

I felt he was communicating with me literally from beyond the grave, telling me that it was all right to be sad, to be angry, hurt and in pain, that it wasn't my fault and just was not meant to be. Maybe he knew me too well. Maybe he knew it would be too tortuous a ritual for me, to see him buried in cold earth. Maybe it would have seemed too final. The pain of his loss was difficult enough without that. This way I could remember him as he was. Maybe we had said our goodbyes that day in his house. Maybe a few days later, when I visited his grave alone, I was saying a personal goodbye to him, as he had wanted it.

Each one of us has lost someone close. Death, bereavement, parting is part of the circle of life and although we may not like to talk about it much, at some point in our lives we will be forced to deal with the cruel reality of death. When Don asked me to join him in compiling this book I welcomed the opportunity to explore this sensitive issue and perhaps in the process bring some clarity to my own experience.

Don and I first met when we wrote separate books on the tour of the relics of St Thérèse in Ireland in 2001, an extraordinary event that captured the imagination of the whole country and from that friendship the seeds of this book were sown on a lazy afternoon in the now extinct Bewley's café in Westmoreland Street, Dublin.

Both of us had heard amazing stories of people who claimed to have experienced inexplicable incidents relating to contact from their deceased loved ones and this fascinated us. It was while talking that we realised that we too had, like

173

so many others, often wondered about the reality of such incidents and it got us thinking. Did these things really happen? Did they mean anything? Or were they simply manifested by the grief-stricken minds of those suffering a great loss?

When we cast out the net asking people to share their experiences with us, we were pleasantly surprised by the response. We made a conscious decision not to engage with psychics, mediums or clairvoyants as we felt it would not allow the book to reach our target audience – ordinary rational people who have lost someone and feel that that person is still with them because of a certain incident, in some cases a vision, a graphic dream, a familiar voice or an event that they simply cannot find a explanation for.

This book therefore was never about the living trying to contact the dead but rather spontaneous communication from the dead to the living. As stories began to arrive however we discovered it would be principally about hope and finding comfort in small things. In turn it is our hope that many, including the bereaved, will find consolation from reading other people's stories.

As more and more testimonies came through the letterbox we quickly realised that this was in fact a global phenomenon. We received letters from literally every corner of Ireland, from England, Scotland, Wales, France, Portugal, Japan and all parts of the USA and Canada, South Africa and Australia. They told stories they had never told before for fear of being ridiculed. Like us, our correspondents had been searching for answers to inexplicable occurrences.

Recognising the sensitivity of the emotions involved and the privilege of presenting people's personal experiences, we felt it only right that the contributors should tell their stories in their own words and in their own style, with a limited amount of editing. We also understood that for many the process of relating the story was therapeutic; for others because it was a difficult and uncomfortable subject we have respected their requests to protect their anonymity.

We have had no shortage of responses to our request for stories relating to contact from the deceased. Some are similar, but each as individual as the person who penned them.

Having read such personal and heartfelt testimonies are we really any closer to discovering the truth? The truth is of course that much as we want to believe in the existence of after-death communication, the reality is that we really cannot be sure it exists until such time as we pass over ourselves.

The task of processing this book was at times a physically and emotionally demanding one. Now, as the end product finally comes to fruition we find ourselves surrounded by page upon page of hand-written and carefully typed correspondence from literally every corner of the world. Between the lines on each and every page we are extended an invitation into a moving and deeply private world. The grief and tears of broken-hearted people pour from these letters like a dam released. Hearts were opened, souls were exposed and inexplicable stories were related, some for the first time in decades. Bereaved men, women and children, those who had lost husbands, wives, children, parents and siblings all related their immense losses with pain and hope and at times the responsibility of dealing with this privileged information was challenging. However the fact that so many complete strangers responded to our request to talk about their closest relationships and the aftermath of loss encouraged us to continue.

As Don and I come to the end of this remarkable journey we find ourselves reflecting on our own experiences once again. My own is something that has intrigued me for many years and to this day I am amazed at the impact that one person has had on my life. It makes me wonder even more about the ripple effect of my friend Larry's life and subsequent death. The loss of such a friend and its effect on me was ultimately instrumental in my participation in this book.

I am comforted but not surprised to find that so many people have had similar experiences. I still wonder if after death communication really does exist or if in the midst of anguish and grief we cling to every little thing in the hope that our deceased loved ones are sending us a sign? On reflection I believe it's the latter but I'm not an authority on the subject. I truly believe that if the incidents recounted in this book bring hope and comfort to those who experienced them first hand then they are valid and significant and worthy of documentation.

Interviews

In order to present a fair and balanced view of an emotive subject we felt that having obtained hundreds of statements from members of the public we should also seek the insight of various experts with a professional view on the topic.

Two of the most intriguing interviews I carried out were with well-known priest and broadcaster Fr Brian D'Arcy and one with Dr Michael Corry, a psychiatrist. Dr Corry is a rational and intelligent man who deals with science and for whom the supernatural has never been a point of focus. I was impressed with his attitude and his honesty and also with his matter of fact way of dealing with a world we know very little about. Dr Corry told me that on average three to four people a month present to him with stories of contact from deceased loved ones. In some cases this contact is unwanted, in others it gives people something positive to cling to in the midst of overwhelming grief. Dr Corry firmly believes that the prevalence of after-death communication is a common one and that those who claim to have these experiences are not unstable but simply struggling to cope with the pain of separation.

In his contribution Fr D'Arcy also acknowledges the reality of contact and, in fact, believes that his own late parents help guide him through life. He also offers a frank insight into the views of the Catholic Church on this topic.

I also spoke to a bereavement counsellor who had a simple approach to the topic: 'If these people loved you in life, why would they abandon you in death?'

Dublin-based psychiatrist Dr Michael Corry is a man who has been trained to evaluate life through science and fact, yet the prevalence of people visiting his surgery claiming to have experienced after death communication has made him reevaluate his beliefs. He now has a number of people attending him because of such communication, on a monthly basis. 'The intense emotions of the bereaved, the seriously distressed and those with extra sensory perception can connect them to the energies of the deceased,' he told me, 'and we should not be surprised at these communications as they arise, transcending as they do non-local consciousness, space and time.

'In some cases people are emotionally distressed relative to a grief; in others people are very emotionally distressed but not because of grief; and the third scenario is where people simply have extra sensory perceptions and their ability to perceive the non-physical is more evolved than the rest of us. Obviously when you're talking about this kind of thing you're moving into another realm and another dimension where all of this is truly possible.

'Many of these people,' explains Dr Curry, 'come to see me with a history of stress of some kind. Sometimes they would tell me about the communication voluntarily but after a while you begin to get a sense of what's going on and you can tell which stories are authentic.' Those who attend the consultant have been bereaved in some way and their loss continues to impact heavily on their lives. 'A man came to see me whose son was killed while cycling to school to do the repeat Leaving Certificate. The father of the boy had made a pact with him. He had promised to buy him a set of drums if

178

he went back to school to do his exams and after the boy was killed his father would hear movement in the bedroom and hear him playing on the drum kit. His son would come downstairs and give him a goodnight kiss on the cheek. He would hear him.'

The man was in great turmoil and visited Dr Corry on a number of occasions, having been referred by his GP who recognised that his emotional state was negatively impacting on his physical state. 'He had suffered an awful lot of stress and his whole immune system had crashed,' continues Dr Corry, who adds that the man was experiencing confusing emotions relating to the apparent presence of his son in the aftermath of his death. 'On one level he was very comfortable with it and happy that his son was alive in a sense and quite ambivalent about the notion that he might be holding back his energy but on another level he recognised that he needed to let go. He worked in the city centre and couldn't physically drive past the cemetery where his son was buried,' said Dr Corry. 'Instead he would take a roundabout way into work.'

Acknowledging a need to move on, the man accepted the consultant's offer of help and was receptive to a plan he had drawn up with this purpose specifically in mind. 'I put in place a very simple ritual which involved the father actually going to the graveyard and facing up to what he had been afraid of, then reading out to his son a letter in which he told him how much he missed him. Together the parents of the boy set fire to the letter,' explains Dr Corry. The grief stricken parents, he said, had effectively created a shrine to their deceased son in his bedroom. 'The clothes their son had worn when he was killed had been dry-cleaned and left in the room untouched and we decided that these should be given away and the room repainted. That was very stressful for the family. To finally get closure, I asked them to contact a religious minister, who would have an awareness of such activity, to come in and say a specific religious ritual meaningful to the faith of those experiencing such contact – in this case, a Mass – aimed at clearing the house and moving the energy on.'

Another incident Dr Corry related involved a man whose son committed suicide in his late teens. The young man had been the victim of sexual abuse during childhood and hanged himself in the attic of his house. His parents came to see Dr Corry because they were greatly disturbed by the continuous presence of their deceased son in the house. They sensed him there all the time, both hearing and seeing him. They simply couldn't handle it. They eventually sold the house and moved away but said that their son began to visit them there as well. In order to deal with this Dr Corry devised a similar plan to that of the first case. 'We went through a similar ritual and had a ceremony performed in the house. That seemed to do the trick but the father came to see me again recently and said that his son was standing at Heuston railway station waiting for him to get off the train every morning when he went to work.' This case has not yet been resolved.

Another instance involves the death of a third young man. 'A man was sent to me by his place of work because he was very depressed but he really didn't want to see me or engage me in conversation at all,' relates Dr Corry. 'At a later stage both he and his wife came to see me and I told them I was aware that they had lost a son in the past. After a while they started to talk about the fact that they could sense their son around the house, in the car and in the garage.'

Intrigued, Dr Corry asked the couple if they sensed their son in the surgery and they pointed to an empty chair and said he was there. 'It was the first time that I'd ever sat in a room with an apparent spirit,' said Dr Corry. 'I looked to the empty chair as though I could see the boy and we had to ne-gotiate a way to ask him if he wanted to be there or if his parents were holding him back. His parents said that the boy had admitted that they were holding him back. He was ready to move on and they were ready to let him, so we worked out a formula which again involved a Mass being said in the house and giving away his clothes to a charity. That achieved some sort of closure for the couple.'

Each case is different however and one young lady had a very different experience after a night out which ended in horror. 'This young woman was going out with a girlfriend to a nightclub when a man pulled up in his car and they got in. He pulled out a knife and tied the girls up. He then raped each a number of times. He threatened to kill them but somehow they managed to beg for their lives and talk him out of kill-ing them. He threw them out of the car and they went to a garda station but one of the girls couldn't give a lot of detail about what had happened and she came to see me, to try and get over the trauma. She told me that what had actually happened was that when she realised that she might die, she went "out of body" and was looking down on the whole scenario when her grandmother, who had died three weeks previously, came to her and held her and said "You're going to be OK", over and over again.'

When asked if such alleged incidents are simply the human psyche playing tricks on vulnerable people in the depths of grief or trauma, Dr Corry answers with an emphatic no. 'These are real stories and involve people whose energies are more receptive to the energies of the deceased. I have come to know when stories are authentic or not. Originally I had no awareness of this at all but after listening to all these stories, I developed an interest. I had to reevaluate my scientific training and come to see that it has implicit limitations with respect to the understanding of consciousness and its infinite interconnectedness. Science is a product of consciousness and therefore cannot have dominance over it. Rather than consciousness being seen within science it is only logical that it has to be science within consciousness. The notion that that which cannot be measured does not exist, is one of enormous conceit. Science is nothing but a tool "a means of gathering information according to the instruments used". After you have listened to enough contact stories and experienced them as authentic, you begin to build up a picture of the non-physical and the spirit energies that reside there.'

Having received a large percentage of testimonies from the USA I decided to consult with Daena Smoller of the International Society for Paranormal Research (ISPR) located in Los Angeles. Smoller studies parapsychology and has participated in paranormal field research.

'In my nine years of experience, I have dealt with those who are still fearful of interaction with a deceased loved one and others who welcome such communication,' says Smoller. 'Paranormal activity from a stranger however, tends to be more disconcerting for the majority of people who encounter such activities.'

As for the reasons why the deceased might make contact, Smoller says they are wide and varied. 'Those who have died and are no longer bound to a physical body, whether they are earthbound or not, can communicate with living individuals. Their reason or reasons for doing so can vary greatly and, truthfully, can be as unique as each individual.'

For Smoller, the existence of an afterlife is without doubt. As to what form it takes, that's a deeper question. 'What exactly the afterlife is, I can't say with any certainty, only that it doesn't appear to be something that can be explained through one description or through a single person's vantage point.'

Sr Anne is a bereavement counsellor working in the Irish midlands. In the course of her work, she has encountered various stories of a 'supernatural' nature. 'We question these kinds of stories and I wouldn't dismiss any of them. I believe that what could be interpreted as coincidences are not – they happen for a reason. When people talk of such coincidences I think they really do happen, although, when people are bereaved, they're in shock, and they often do irrational things,' she says. 'We often find that in the case of someone with a terminal illness, people wait for their loved ones to leave the room before they die because they don't want to cause them pain and then they make it up to them by contacting them at a later stage. We've also heard from a woman whose brother died suddenly and when she was in his garden she says she got a lovely scent of flowers and believes it was him.

'These are all inexplicable incidents and I don't know how to rationalise them but I wouldn't dismiss them and they obviously bring comfort to a lot of people. People desperately want to believe. When you're heartbroken you will cling to anything. I think the deceased can communicate with the living when they are at peace. If someone loves you in life, why would they abandon you in death?' she asks.

In the USA spiritual consultant Barbara Mallon is actively involved in the exploration of the paranormal and the existence of life after death communication. She believes that she has been chosen as a communicator between the deceased and the living. She sets out to gain as much information as she can from the deceased, to pass onto the living, so that they understand exactly who is trying to connect with them. Through her work, Mallon claims to have become a stronger and more positive person. 'I've had glimpses of the spirit world. I've learned and experienced the tremendous sense of peace one has after they recognise and identify the spirit person communicating with me, etc. and I've discovered that our deceased loved ones are right here with us and around us and work hard to do little things to let us know they're around,' she says.

Many of the experiences in this book are ones of comfort and reassurance but what of those who feel such communication is an unwelcome imposition in their lives? What if such incidents leave people feeling afraid or unsure? Mallon believes that paranormal activity can be a worry for people only if they feel unable to understand it. 'I try to educate people about how deceased people connect with us, so they can acknowledge the activity rather than brushing it off as their imagination or becoming afraid,' she explains. 'If something does scare you or you don't like this kind of activity from either a loved one or anyone, just tell them to stop. If they don't stop, they probably are not your loved one in spirit, but rather another energy, and you may need to spiritually cleanse your home. Our spirit loved ones do not try to scare us.'

Mallon's belief is that when we die, we change from a physical form into a spirit form. In this capacity, the deceased let us know they're around all of the time in quite a few different ways. As to the reasons for such attempted communication, she asks us to imagine how it might feel to be away from our loved ones, yet safe and at peace. 'Wouldn't you want to try to connect with your people here on earth, to let them know you are near, see them, ease their pain, and so on?' she asks. 'Most of the time, we just feel these spirit people right next to us; we feel their presence; we know it's them just by their feeling. Sometimes, we feel them walk right through us. We can even smell them or feel them once again when this happens.'

As for convincing others of the reality of after-death communication, Mallon says she doesn't push her opinions on anyone and allows people to make up their own minds on the subject. 'I just deliver the messages, or become the channel for doing so. I know there is an afterlife. It's very normal to me, as are our God-given abilities.'

Though not categorically accepting the existence of after death communication, well known priest and broadcaster Fr Brian D'Arcy is not ruling it out either.

'Life and death are both mysteries and nobody knows all the answers but it would seem to me that the Church's teaching has always been that there is a possibility of us influencing the lives of those who have gone before and indeed of them influencing us. This is called the Communion of Saints', he says in reference to the quote, 'Our prayer for them is capable not only of helping them, but also of making their intercession for us effective', which can be found in the most recent catechism of the Catholic Church.

The Church as an institution, he says, holds mixed views on the issue and is unlikely to state officially that any particular event was truly a communication from beyond the grave. However, he continues, 'Anybody working in the pastoral field will also recognise that death is not the end. Put simply the Catholic Church believes that those who die in God's grace and friendship and are perfectly purified live forever with Christ. They are like God forever, for they see him as he is, face to face.

'People who live with God can and do communicate in various ways with those who are still on earth,' maintains Fr D'Arcy, drawing on his own personal experiences. 'Without a doubt I would know that my own parents constantly look after me, care for me and indeed intervene in events of life to carry me safely through. That's why we pray to our parents and those who loved us, as well as praying for them.'

The Enniskillen-based priest is 'not in the least bit surprised' at the incredible response this book has generated and says it points to a greater awareness of the process of grieving. 'It shows that as people become more aware of the grieving process, they become more aware too of the influence of those who have died. They have been part of their lives for so long that death itself cannot stop them from being part of their lives in the future. Each person has their own way of communicating and of reading the signs of the times. Nobody else has to know it, nobody else has to be convinced,' he says, 'but the people themselves knows when their loved one who is dead is looking after them.'

However if there is a danger, continues Fr D'Arcy, it is that individuals overwhelmed by loss may in some way subconsciously experience seemingly inexplicable incidents, so desperate are they to believe that their deceased loved ones are still with them in some way. In this instance, he warns, alleged after death communication could become an unhealthy intrusion in one's life. 'This is why it's very important to have somebody else to help you work your way through these events,' he says. 'Grief counselling is very important and it is imperative that we be sensible about these things because it is very easy to go from accepting that those who are gone before us can help us, to allowing them in some unhealthy way to take over our lives. That is a difficulty. I believe personally that a mother or father or a loved one who dies helps us from their place in God's kingdom. They do direct our thoughts. They don't however take over our will or take away our free will. They prod, direct, help us in the same way as the living do, but at the end of the day we are responsible for our own decisions and for our own choices. Nobody takes that away from us,' he stresses.

Where people have clearly been helped or comforted by what they believe to be communication from a deceased loved one, Fr D'Arcy says it can only be a good thing if it helps ease the pain of loss. 'I have been quite aware of being helped by people who have died and I've known many people who get great comfort from that fact,' he says. 'They know little signs which are not disturbing but which encourage people that they are being looked after in a special way and indeed drawn to God by what they do.

'Maybe that is the key to it all,' he reflects. 'If we are being drawn to goodness, to life, to happiness and to peace then those are gifts which God would like us to have. If we are being drawn to distress, despair, unhappiness and fragility, those are not good gifts and are not from God.'

Perhaps we should return to psychiatrist Dr Michael Corry

for a final word. 'Science has yet to catch up and embrace the obvious fact: that there is much more unknown than known.'

A good conclusion to the book.

AUDREY HEALY
Co-author
Longford, Ireland, August 2005

We would like to extend an invitation to people everywhere to continue to submit their experiences with a view to publication. Please send to: Audrey Healy, c/o Mercier Press, Douglas Village, Cork, Ireland. Alternatively email:

yourstory@eircom.net